A Practical Guide to Cosmetic Surgery Claims

Dr Victoria R Handley
Solicitor, Director of Handley Law Ltd
LLB (Hons), LLM, Dip PI Lit, PhD
Solicitors For Women
Clinical Negligence, Cosmetic Surgery, Personal Injury, Care Home Negligence

Law Brief Publishing

Published 2017 by
Law Brief Publishing
30 The Parks
Minehead
Somerset
TA24 8BT

www.lawbriefpublishing.com

Paperback: 978-1-911035-27-5

PREFACE

Most cosmetic procedures take well people, make them sick and then hope that they will look better when they recover. Cosmetic surgery is big business. Whilst 2016 may have had the lowest numbers in the UK for a decade, it was still 31,000 procedures according to the British Association of Aesthetic Plastic Surgeons. Abdominoplasty surgery remained popular for both genders. The increase in male abdominoplasty is because there is no adequate non-surgical option for the removal of excess skin. With Britons' shedding weight either through diet, exercise or bariatric surgery, the numbers show that men are keen to use surgical methods to complete the process.

Women's breast augmentation surgery continues to remain the most popular procedure. Smaller sizes are now more fashionable than oversized breasts of the past. Women are looking for a more natural enhancement. Whether there is a successful outcome is largely in the mind of the patient, the consent process and the skill of the surgeon. Whether the result is good depends upon the expectation of the patient.

Manufacturers are required to design and manufacture medical devices in such a way that, when the devices are used under the conditions and for the purposes intended, they will not compromise the clinical condition or the safety of patients. This is provided any risks which may be associated with the intended surgery constitute acceptable risks when weighed against the benefits to the patient. Yet so often these can go wrong.

There are three elements to successful cosmetic surgery, patient selection, a skilled surgeon and truly informed consent. When these are present the patient can be satisfied that the treatment has been done well. Subsequent surgeries pose additional risks. Many patients fail to appreciate that, for many cosmetic procedures such as breast implants, it is the start of a journey which requires removal and replacement every 10 years or so. Fillers and Botox require additional treatments at regular intervals. For the surgeon, it is a customer for life. For the patient, it is a financial commitment to maintain the desired result which carries additional risk with each application.

The US Institute of Medicine's report *To Err is Human* (1999) was the first to highlight that too many inpatients were coming to unnecessary harm with deaths in hospitals from preventable adverse events exceeding those from breast cancer or road accidents. Since then there have been numerous reports and policies to reduce unintended or unexpected incidents which lead to harm. Much work has been done to create a culture of safety worldwide. The cosmetic surgery industry is no exception to experiencing adverse incidents. Patient safety is not exclusively an NHS issue. It is important for all surgeons and treatment specialists to know their patient and pay attention to detail when administering any treatment.

Yet things do go wrong and frequently. Patients often complain initially because they want an explanation of what happened, an assurance it won't happen again and an apology. The majority of complaints can be resolved quickly. However, repeat or corrective surgeries are not always in the patient's best interests and can lead to further harm and complications.

People have been modifying themselves for centuries in the pursuit of beauty. Now, more than ever before, images in magazines and press as well as social media, fuel the concept of what is beautiful. We live in a society obsessed with looks. Yet many women undergoing cosmetic surgery do not tell their family or friends about the decision. They have the surgery to correct perceived inadequacies. Whilst unhappy people are unlikely to make themselves happy with cosmetic surgery it is nevertheless, a path chosen by thousands and the demand for procedures is likely to continue.

The sector is highly fragmented encompassing a range of procedures, from relatively minor interventions to major surgery. There is a wide range of different groups, including medical device manufacturers, doctors and those who provide clinics and facilities, and there is no single professional or trade organisation that represents all these groups. There is no quality control. Existing legislation has developed in a piecemeal fashion, addressing certain aspects of the sector but not taking a systematic approach. Attempts at self-regulation have largely failed because of the diversity of the sector and competition within it.

There are few books written about cosmetic surgery litigation. Sections can be found in clinical negligence books as the principles are the same. This is a look at the litigation environment in the UK relating to cosmetic surgery. It is produced to facilitate an understanding of cosmetic surgery claims for the busy practitioner. Whilst the book concentrates on surgical cosmetic treatments, many of the principles can equally apply to non-surgical procedures and other beauty treatments which have an adverse outcome. From breast surgery to Botox, informed consent, alternative treatments and negligently carrying out the treatment causing loss remains the same.

Throughout we have referred to 'cosmetic surgery litigation'. The term is intended to include pre-litigation considerations and regulation. The principles can apply to invasive and non-invasive treatments alike. Cosmetic surgery is booming business and marketing is slick and ruthless. The opposition is formidable in terms of their understanding of business and risk. Some of the best consent forms have been constructed to contain a bucket list of what can go wrong, precisely because some of the people who seek cosmetic surgery don't consider risk as a factor in the journey to a better body. Some clinics fail to carry insurance and many (following the PIP Breast Implant Scandal) fold and set up the next day without carrying over their liabilities.

Such complex litigation can provide a challenge for the practitioner but it is a rewarding area of law. When cosmetic surgery goes wrong it can go horribly wrong and to be able to offer guidance and redress is the very reason the tort system exists. We as practitioners are privileged to use the law to facilitate access to justice for those clients.

The book covers the regulation of Defendants, product liability and negligence claims. Medical devices and compensation including particular risks of various procedures. This is a reflection of the UK market as at March 2017. As new procedures are developed patients will continue to be injured, some horribly. As new information emerges and consumer awareness grows new litigation areas may emerge. As the Government looks at the small claims limit and introduction of fixed fees in clinical negligence claims, practitioners face uncertain times.

Victoria Handley
April 2017

Contents

CHAPTER ONE
WHAT IS COSMETIC SURGERY?

Cosmetic surgery is where a person chooses to have an operation or invasive medical procedure, to change their physical appearance for cosmetic rather than medical reasons. We refer to cosmetic surgery as any intervention, procedure or treatment carried out with the primary objective of changing an aspect of a patient's physical appearance. This includes surgical and non-surgical procedures, both invasive and non-invasive. Non-surgical procedures such as Botox or dermal fillers, typically used to relax or fill crease lines, do not involve surgery but there are still risks attached.

Cosmetic surgery is rarely available on the NHS unless there is an overriding physical or psychological reason. The majority therefore have surgery carried out privately. The NHS will not help if it goes wrong unless there is a serious complication which means that emergency or life-saving treatment is necessary.

If we consider the most heavily regulated surgical invasive procedures and understand the burdens on the treatment provider, documents they must have and disclose and consent; we can apply the same principles to all cosmetic treatments. The cause of action for a cosmetic surgery claim can arise via legislation (Consumer Protection Act) or common law negligence.

The Patient vs Profit

The cosmetic surgery industry is worth approximately £3.6 billion. It has expanded at such a rate that regulation is glaringly inadequate. Competition for clients is high. To attract new patients the marketing strategies of cosmetic surgery clinics and doctors are slick and persuasive. Botulinum toxins and hyaluronic acid fillers account for the majority of non-surgical cosmetic procedures. The aim of cosmetic surgery clinics is to have a strong relationship with the clients so they will keep coming back, often every 3-4 months and so will their friends. Word of mouth is a good way to establish the practice and quality training will keep them coming back. Referrals bring loyal clients and the foundation of trust with successful treatments means long term clients.

Having surgery is a big decision and its' based on a dissatisfaction with appearance. Surgical cosmetic procedures are on the increase both in number and type. It is possible to cosmetically alter the majority of your body. Certain procedures are one off whilst others (implants) will need to be removed and replaced in time. The procedures are however expensive. Many clients take out loans or pay on credit cards.

Websites and social media platforms allow clinics to market directly to their key audience. People considering surgery want as much information as they can get and recommendations or good feedback is key. Clinics attract patients by writing educational materials, feature articles, advertorial in newspapers or magazines, books and blogs sharing experiences. Many are written by allegedly 'ex-patients' making recommendations about the care they received. Online forums discuss issues emotively and offer solutions, special offers and vouchers. Clinics are persuasive 'they only offer safe treatments that deliver results', the 'guarantee scheme' helps build trust. They only ever work with the 'industry's best doctors, surgeons or nurses'. They 'continually invest in technology which combined with the superior skill of the doctors, delivers the best results'. They 'care about their patients and their satisfaction'. They state that 'patient safety is a priority'. Best of all 'as seen on TV'. For a patient considering surgery, all boxes are ticked.

Aggressive marketing and ruthless sales tactics of some unscrupulous companies mean that it is very difficult for patients to find independent, trustworthy information to inform them as to what an operation would entail. Undergoing cosmetic surgery is a big decision. A patient should never feel rushed or pressured into getting surgery by a third party. They should not be pressed to proceed because of special offers which are time limited, discounts or two for one deals. Surgery should not be offered as a prize. Marketing must be factual, clear and not misleading.

The decision by a clinic or doctor to operate and accept a patient as a customer should be considered carefully. In some situations it is clear that the patient should not have the desired procedure. This is not patient autonomy being overruled by defensive medicine. There is an increasing trend towards multiple surgeries which carry additional risks. It may seem attractive to the patient to have one procedure to fix all. It may seem attractive to the surgeon to be paid for carrying out multiple surgeries in one sitting. Nevertheless, the combined risk factors, level of monitoring needed during and post-surgery and the inherent driver to have so many procedures done at the same time should sound alarm bells. A surgeon should politely decline but the fear that the patient will take the considerable sum of money elsewhere often overrules good sense.

Seeking a psychological profile of the patient before cosmetic procedures are carried out seems like a good way of determining the right patient for the right procedure. But, how much can we really know about the psychological issues related to individuals? Who is suitably qualified to carry out the psychological profiling and what indeed is the overall correct outcome if someone displays psychological issues? Various studies have taken place in the US and Canada which have shown that there is a slightly higher risk (just over twice that found in the general population) of suicide among women with breast implants. Quite why is unknown. In contrast to women in the general population, women with implants have significantly lower body mass indices, greater likelihoods of cigarette smoking, more induced abortions and fewer live births, lower educational levels and more screenings for breast disease. Is this more reflective of who they are rather than a link between suicide and implants? Should this influence the choice of procedure at all?

Whilst psychological profiling can identify issues, what is expected to happen with the data? There may be a clear reason identified to say no to further procedures. Identifying and classifying body dysmorphia (BDD) for instance, is not the role of a cosmetic surgeon. BDD occurs in 1% of the general population. If an individual has a pre-occupation with an imagined defect in appearance, isn't that the subjective nature of cosmetic surgery procedures in any event? A client may be dissatisfied with their appearance and seek treatment. A surgeon may think the client looks fine. At what point is the surgeon wrong to undergo treatment if it is what the client wants after considering the risks and complications? Equally, the patient who has seen several surgeons because they have failed to produce the desired result: are they ever going to find the desired result? Does it exist and can additional surgery with additional scarring seek to achieve it?

It is an interesting discussion and it is raised to highlight the argument that psychological profiling can have. Many clinics have a questionnaire completed by nurses setting out the reasons for seeking surgery. They are likely to encounter increasing numbers of patients who are seeking cosmetic surgery and who have psychological issues or psychiatric comorbidities. Being alert to specific psychiatric disorders will enhance proper diagnosis and one may expect cosmetic surgeons not to undertake treatments. Quite how they are to deliver their diagnosis of psychological illness when they are not qualified to do so is interesting.

The chances of a patient encountering poor quality products, poor quality treatment, and poor quality aftercare is surprisingly high – and for non-surgical procedures, there is no guarantee of redress. Treatments carried out which are non-surgical have less regulation. Doctors are regulated by the General Medical Council but individuals have no such professional duty.

Regulation

Thought has been given to restricting cosmetic interventions carried out by doctors, nurses, and others, who are not appropriately qualified or indemnified to do so. There is a need to help patients find redress when things go wrong. The Department of Health's report into the *Review of Regulation of Cosmetic Interventions* was asked to review regulation in the cosmetic interventions sector following the PIP implant scandal which exposed 'woeful lapses in product quality, aftercare and record keeping'. It also drew attention to widespread use of 'misleading advertising, inappropriate marketing and unsafe practices right across the sector'. It recommended:

- A register of everyone who performs surgical or non-surgical cosmetic interventions
- Classifying dermal fillers as a prescription only medical device

- Ensuring all practitioners are properly qualified for all the procedures they offer
- All non-surgical procedures must be performed under the responsibility of a clinical professional who has gained the accredited qualification to prescribe, administer and supervise aesthetic procedures
- A ban on special financial offers for surgery
- An advertising code of conduct with mandatory compliance for practitioners
- Compulsory professional indemnity in case things go wrong
- An ombudsman to oversee all private healthcare, including cosmetic procedures, to help those who have been treated poorly.

The Cosmetic Surgery (Minimum Standards Bill) 2012-2013 was drafted to establish minimum standards for the practice of cosmetic surgery, including non-surgical procedures. The Bill was designed to set up an Implant registry, establish the Cosmetic Surgery Regulatory and Standards Authority, seek the prohibition of advertising cosmetic surgery and cosmetic intervention procedures, clarify offences and identify non-surgical cosmetic intervention procedures. In 2013 it failed to complete its passage through Parliament before the end of the session which means the Bill will make no further progress.

According to the *Review of Regulation of Cosmetic Interventions*, the current regulatory framework places 'no restrictions on who may perform nonsurgical cosmetic procedures. No qualifications are required to carry out these procedures and, in the absence of accredited training courses, anyone can set up a training course purporting to offer a qualification. There are a number of self-accredited training organisations but none are regulated'.

The **Royal College of Surgeons** guidance, *Professional Standards for Cosmetic Practice*, stated that 'only licensed doctors, registered dentists and registered nurses should provide any cosmetic treatments (including laser treatments and injectable cosmetic treatments)'. However, there is no legislation that will make indemnity or insurance for all practitioners become obligatory.

When things go wrong and you are instructed by a client who has undertaken a cosmetic procedure which they are unhappy with it is important to identify who the Defendant is and how they may be regulated.

Check that the hospital or clinic is registered with the **Care Quality Commission** (CQC). If they are not registered they may be practising illegally and their insurance may not cover them or the patient if something goes wrong. By law a clinic or hospital must register with the CQC if they offer:

- Cosmetic surgery involving instruments or equipment being inserted into the body (including implants)
- Laser lipolysis (such as Smart Lipo)
- Refractive eye surgery or lens implant surgery

They do not regulate:

- Subcutaneous muscle relaxing injections for improving appearance such as Botox
- Dermal fillers
- Chemical peels
- Laser and intense pulse light treatments like hair removal or skin rejuvenation
- Procedures that do not involve cutting or inserting instruments or equipment into the body

Check the inspection reports from the CQC to ascertain prior concerns for the clinic or hospital. There may be prior concerns highlighted which are prudent to the case at hand.

BAPRAS & BAAPS

Check whether the surgeon is a full and accredited member of BAPRAS (British Association of Plastic Reconstructive and Aesthetic Surgeons) or BAAPS The British Association of Aesthetic Plastic Surgeons.

Failing to become a member of recognised organisations or listing a different specialism to that undertaken in the patient's case can be indicative of the type of defendant that you are dealing with. There is no requirement to be registered but patients would be wise to only undertake surgery from a doctor registered with these associations as a starting point.

General Medical Council

Check the General Medical Council register. There are about 245,000 doctors on the UK medical register. Doctors who provide cosmetic surgery independently in the private sector only need to be registered as a doctor. They do not have to be listed as a specialist surgeon on the GMC's specialist register.

The GMC ensures that for every doctor who joins the register there are no concerns about behaviour, health or performance that could prevent them from doing their job. Once a doctor is on the register there are a series of checks called 'revalidation' that occur once every five years. Revalidation is the process whereby doctors are required to demonstrate that they are up to date and fit to practice in accordance with their professional standards. They must collect information about their practice including feedback from patients, have an annual appraisal based on the guidance 'Good Medical Practice' and reflect and consider improvements that they could make. Revalidation makes sure that every licensed doctor has an annual appraisal.

If a doctor poses an ongoing risk, they can have their practice restricted or suspended (whilst they retrain say). On occasion, a doctor is not allowed back to work because their conduct was so serious. They can be removed from the register or 'struck off'.

Some doctors fly into the UK to perform cosmetic surgery. They are not registered with the GMC. Some clinics fly patients out of the country to undergo cosmetic procedures. In both instances, the patient is not afforded the protection that they would get in the UK.

The **GMC** published *'Guidance for Doctors who offer Cosmetic Interventions'* in April 2016 which incorporated principles from existing guidance but went further. It set a higher standard to address the specific safety issues and ethical concerns of the cosmetic sector following the recommendations of **Sir Bruce Keogh's** ***Review of the Regulation of Cosmetic Interventions***. It is prudent to read the guidance and use it when reviewing medical records, instructing experts to comment on adherence to professional duties, reviewing witness statements and drafting Part 18 questions.

Throughout the guidance, the terms 'you must' and 'you should' are used. 'You must' is used for an overriding duty or principle. 'You should' is used when providing an explanation of how a doctor will meet the overriding duty. It is also used where the duty or principle will not apply in all situations or circumstances, or where there are factors outside a doctor's control that affect whether or how they can follow the guidance. Thus, all documents in the case can be checked against the overriding duty to ensure compliance with the professional standards. Any omission will strengthen the patients case.

The **Royal College of Surgeons** has also produced guidance on the professional standards, skills and experience needed to carry out cosmetic interventions (*Professional Standards for Cosmetic Surgery* (2016)). Taking the recommendations of the review by the Department of Health into the regulation of cosmetic interventions following the publication of Professional Standards for Cosmetic Practice (RCS, 2013), the Royal College of Surgeons and the Cosmetic Surgery Interspecialty Committee (CSIC) developed a certification scheme. The aim was to provide evidence of competences (including professional behaviours, clinical skills, knowledge and experience in defined areas of cosmetic surgery. The guidance addressed key areas of risk identified for cosmetic surgery including 'communication, consent, professional behaviours and dealing with a psychologically vulnerable patient'. Space does not permit the full reproduction of this important document. You are encouraged to read it and keep it to hand for every communication and review of your file. Your expert should refer to the standards when considering the medical notes and consent documents.

Cosmetic surgery is often advertised online and by email. The marketing tactics put pressure on the recipient to sign a contract to avail of a deal. Promotional tactics should not be used to encourage people to make an ill-considered decision but nevertheless they do. The patient should be advised about any financial or commercial interests that could be seen to affect the doctor's advice. The purchase of goods and services over the internet, by telephone or by email order are generally subject to consumer protection regulations. On 13 June 2014, the Consumer Contracts (Information, Cancellation and Additional Charges) Regulations 2013 replaced the Consumer Protection (Distance Selling) Regulations 2000 and Cancellation of Contracts made in a Consumer's Home or Place of Work etc Regulations 2008. The regulations set out pre-contractual information that should be provided to a consumer, depending on whether the contract is made on or off premises eg: main characteristics of the goods or services, identity of trader, total price including tax.

The **Committee of Advertising Practice** has developed guidance on the advertising and *Marketing of Cosmetic Interventions.*

Check also:

Qualification Requirements for Delivery of Cosmetic Procedures and *Report on Implementation of Qualification Requirements for Cosmetic Procedures* both by NHS Health Education England.

The **Private Healthcare Information Network** (PHIN) provides a search function to 'compare different hospitals. It is independent and not for profit and works with organisations across the UK including NHS, care quality regulators, government information sources, the medical profession and independent hospitals'. All providers of private healthcare in the UK, including most NHS hospitals, are required by law to submit data to PHIN.

Specific Regulation of Procedures

1. Botulinum toxin is regulated as a prescription medicine but it can then be used by a non-health professional.

2. Breast implants are regulated as a medical device and must be performed by a qualified doctor.

3. Chemical peels are regulated under General Product Safety Directive only if sold direct to a consumer. Anyone in the clinic can administer it.

4. Dermal fillers are regulated as devices only if they have an explicit medical purpose. As most don't they can be used by anyone in the clinic to administer to a patient.

5. Laser treatment equipment is regulated as a medical device but again it can be used by anyone in the clinic to administer to a patient.

6. Intense pulsed light is not regulated as a device and again can be used by anyone.

If your client has undergone a non-surgical procedure, then ask questions of the practitioner to determine whether they have the required skill and expertise to undertake the procedure successfully and safely. What training and accreditation process have they undertaken to identify and manage complications of treatment? The curriculum and training should be disclosed and reviewed.

Statutory Duty of Candour

Independent care providers registered with the CQC are subject to a statutory duty of candour. It is defined in the Robert Francis Report as

"The volunteering of all relevant information to persons who have or may have been harmed by the provisions of services, whether or not the information has been requested and whether or not a complaint or a report about that provision has been made" (Francis chaired a public inquiry into how poor care at Mid Staffordshire Foundation Trust was allowed to happen in the period between January 2005 and March 2009, and why none of the organisations responsible for regulating or managing the trust spotted problems sooner. His recommendations following the inquiry are known as the 'Francis Report').

This statutory duty sits alongside existing contractual and ethical duties of candour. Doctors have had a professional duty of candour for many years. In its core guidance for Good Medical Practice (2013) para 55, the GMC says:

"You must be open and honest with patients if things go wrong. If a patient under your care has suffered harm or distress, you should:

a. Put matters right (if that is possible)

b. Offer an apology

c. Explain fully and promptly what has happened and the likely short-term and long-term effects".

The intention of the regulation is to ensure that providers are open and transparent with people who use services and other 'relevant persons' (people acting lawfully on their behalf) in relation to care and treatment. It sets out the basic requirements that providers must follow when things go wrong with care and treatment, including, 'informing people about the incident, providing reasonable support, providing truthful information and an apology when things go wrong'. It applies to registered persons when they are carrying out a regulated activity. As such the CQC can prosecute for a breach of parts 20(2)(a) and 20(3) of the Regulation and can prosecute without first serving a Warning Notice. There are other regulatory actions available to the CQC including 'a summary conviction for a fine not exceeding £2,500'. Where an organisation's clinical governance procedures for reporting and investigating incidents are followed, it is rare for a patient safety incident to be overlooked. In any event, doctors must always follow their ethical duty, irrespective of whether the statutory duty applies.

It is worthy of note that the NHS does not limit the private work undertaken by their surgeons. It is worth checking to see if there are any NHS issues. If the doctor is suspended from practice in the NHS, he or she can still do private work unless the GMC has placed a restriction on his/her licence. If there is a partial restriction they can only do certain procedures.

From a tactical point of view – know your defendant. Find out what work he or she does and how often. How often is the private work carried out? Do they work weekends? Could the surgeon have been too tired? When was the date of surgery? Did they work weekends or evenings in the run up to the surgery? Did they operate with back to back surgeries? How accurately can they recall your patient and the conversations and why?

CHAPTER TWO
INSURANCE

The healthcare professional carrying out the treatment or the clinic should have insurance in case something goes wrong. The surgeon should have insurance to cover private treatment. On occasion, there is no insurance in place. This is either because the doctor did not take it out, it lapsed, or the insurers fail to indemnify.

In some situations the clinics indemnify the doctors in their employ. Some clinics self-insure. Some have no insurance for certain types of claim or at all. Some clinics contend that they do not supply cosmetic surgery but simply introduce the patient to the surgeon and provide the facilities. Thus, if the surgeon makes an error they are not liable.

A surgeon is potentially liable in negligence for injuries caused whether or not they are also liable in contract. The GMC does not keep a record of individual doctors' insurance or indemnity arrangements. For NHS doctors indemnity is provided through the Clinical Negligence Scheme for Trusts (CHST) which is administered by the NHS Litigation Authority. For work outside the NHS additional personal insurance or indemnity for claims is needed. If the non-NHS treatment takes place on NHS premises alternative insurance is needed.

Some independent healthcare providers provide corporate insurance or indemnity but it should not be assumed that this provides adequate protection and indemnity. It is a tactic of some clinics that each party (clinic and doctor) have separate contracts whereby each assume the other is providing the indemnity. The patient may find that upon suing a clinic for vicarious liability of their doctor that the doctor has a separate consultancy contract which indemnifies the clinic for acts or omissions. However, if the negligence involves an implant, you may find that you are faced with 3 possible defendants; the doctor, manufacturer and clinic. Each blaming the other and claiming indemnity. Further complications arise when the clinic has gone bust and no documents are in existence.

For those doctors who undertake non-NHS work in the UK but carry EU wide insurance arranged outside the UK, you need to ascertain whether the EU insurance covers work in the UK. Check it is adequate or appropriate or of sufficient value to cover claims made in the UK. In some instances the insurers deny they have an obligation to indemnify because:

- They have already had a claim on the policy
- It doesn't cover outside of the jurisdiction or
- The insurance has lapsed.

It may sometimes be difficult to find the surgeon who lives abroad, let alone recover compensation through his/her insurer. Establishing the identity and location of the surgeon and insurance early on in the claim, is crucial to establishing whether the case will be successful.

It is a controversial area. Much depends on the terms and conditions in the contract and how it was entered into, but few patients read the small print or consider the complexities of insurance. Complex agreements exist between clinic, surgeon, anaesthetist, nursing staff and providers of equipment. By law goods supplied under contract by a business to an individual should be of satisfactory quality for which the clinic would be liable. Don't assume anything about the relationships of those involved until the contractual position has been established.

When a Cosmetic Surgery Clinic Closes

If the clinic does not have effective insurance and goes into administration, there are usually very little assets with which to meet any legal liability to pay compensation. Following the PIP Implant litigation it became clear that the majority of clinics did not have adequate insurance cover. Some did not have cover at all. Thus, faced with a large number of claims by patients, the clinics went into administration. Patients had nowhere to go to recover compensation. Whilst the clinic may set up the next day with the same service, same surgeons and same care, the restructuring means that it is now a different legal entity and its liabilities have been left behind.

If there is evidence that the company has closed to escape its liabilities, it is possible to write to the liquidators and invite them to pursue a claim for breach of duty against the directors together with a Section 423 Insolvency Act Claim (i.e. the transaction was made at an undervalue). A transaction will be at an undervalue for the purposes of ss 423, 238 and 339 of the Insolvency Act 1986 if the transferor 'receives no consideration or receives consideration the value of which in money or money's worth is significantly less than the value of the consideration provided by the debtor'.

Section 423 of the Insolvency Act 1986 applies to individuals and companies and is of application whether or not there is a formal insolvency. The section allows the court to unscramble transactions entered into at an undervalue with the purpose of 'putting assets beyond the reach of creditors or of otherwise prejudicing the interests of such people'. An application maybe made by the insolvency practitioner in charge of the insolvency or, with the leave of the court, by a victim of the transaction.

A court faced with an application under s 423 of the Insolvency Act 1986 has to consider, first, 'whether the transaction was at an undervalue' and, secondly, 'the purpose of the transaction'. There is no restriction on the amount of time which may have elapsed since the transaction but the longer ago it was, the more difficult it will be to establish the necessary motive. Putting assets out of the reach of a creditor or creditors 'must have been the purpose behind the transaction, not merely the result of it'.

Breach of Contract

Depending on the circumstances in the case and the policy provisions in the contract, it is possible to sue for breach of contract. For instance, if you are unable to obtain a valid copy of the surgeons insurance policy and the clinic maintains that he carries his own indemnity. If you are unable to sue him directly, you may be able to take action against the clinic, alleging that it had failed to carry out appropriate checks on the surgeon. Check the terms of the contract. You need to show that the surgeon/provider breached a term of the contract in order to succeed in the claim.

CHAPTER THREE
CREDIT CARDS

If a patient pays for treatment by credit card, then they are able to recover compensation through the supplier of credit. It is a requirement that the sum must be no less than £100 and no more than £30,000. It must be the Claimant's credit card and the main card (in the event that it is husband and wife).

S.75 Consumer Credit Act

> *75. — (1) If the debtor under a debtor-creditor-supplier agreement falling within section 12(b) or (c) has, in relation to a transaction financed by the agreement, any claim against the supplier in respect of a misrepresentation or breach of contract, he shall have a like claim against the creditor, who, with the supplier, shall accordingly be jointly and severally liable to the debtor.*

The agreement does not have to be in writing. It can be verbal. There is no requirement to take up the matter with the clinic before pursuing the s.75 route. It is not a requirement to exhaust all possible avenues of redress before pursuing a claim. The credit card company has the same responsibility as the retailer if things go wrong. It is to ensure that you are not paying for something that you did not get or is not fit for purpose. A patient can still claim even if they no longer have the credit card. The law also applies to store cards, store instalment credit and some car finance agreements (though not hire purchase). It does not apply to cash withdrawals from credit cards or using Paypal.

A patient is able to claim back the original cost, any additional expenses plus compensation. There must be clear evidence of a breach not just disappointment at the outcome. Sometimes the credit card company will ask for evidence of fault by independent verification. If it asks for this, and then approves the claim, it should also reimburse the costs incurred in getting the expert opinion. Most claims go ahead without this, but it's a possibility the lender will ask.

If the credit supplier refuses to deal with the issue then you can take it, for free to the Financial Ombudsman Service. It can rule, order compensation and even pay for the inconvenience of having to claim. Where a court only looks at the law, the Ombudsman looks at the law, or standard industry practice, or whether the patient has been treated fairly and reasonably. This method was first developed during the PIP breast implant scandal which successfully allowed people to get their money back from credit card providers as the clinics either refused to deal or went into administration.

If there is an issue with implants, such as in the PIP Implant scandal, patients relied on the Sale of Goods Act 1979 (now replaced by the Consumer Rights Act which came into force on 1st October 2015) to make this complaint. This means that the goods (implants) had to be of a satisfactory quality, as described, fit for purpose and last a reasonable length of time. These rules last six years from purchase. In the first six months it's for the company to prove they weren't faulty when bought, after that you must prove they were.

CHAPTER FOUR LITIGATION CONSIDERATIONS

Limitation

Limitation periods impose time limits within which a Claimant must bring a claim, or give notice of a claim to the Defendant. They are imposed by statute, primarily the Limitation Act 1980 ("LA 1980"). There are different limitation periods for different types of cause of action. It is necessary at the outset of any new claim to determine whether or not the limitation period has expired. If it has, the claim will be "statute-barred" and the claimant may be prevented from bringing a claim against the alleged wrongdoer.

If a claim is brought out of time, the defendant will be able to plead the defence of limitation and the claimant will have the burden of proving that the cause of action arose within the relevant statutory period. Time runs from different dates depending upon the cause of action. For example, in a personal injury claim, time will usually run for 3 years from the date when the negligent act or omission occurred. In respect of cosmetic surgery and clinical negligence claims, it is possible to bring a claim outside the three-year limitation period if the damage complained of was not discovered until after the expiry of the three-year limitation period. This extension to the ordinary limitation period means that a claimant has three years from either the date of knowledge of loss or the date when she ought reasonably to have known of her loss. What constitutes "ought reasonably to have known" depends on the circumstances of the case, and specific advice should be sought on that.

There is the 10 year long-stop for the statutory cause of action under the Consumer Protection Act 1987. The 10 year long–stop in s.11A is notably rigid and time may start running (and even expire) before a cause of action has accrued, and so before the primary limitation period has started. Essentially, the time for calculating the long-stop runs from the date of supply under s.4 of the 1987 Act, and is unaffected by 'disability, infancy, or knowledge'. This can happen when the supply of the implant starts the limitation timetable but the implant is not used by the hospital until near 10 years later. This rule was examined in depth in the *O'Byrne v Aventis Pasteur SA* (26.05.10) case when the ECJ judgment confirmed that the 10 year long-stop period remained. UK manufacturers have certainty about the period of time in which they may face liability under the Consumer Product Act and the Product Liability Directive and thus they cannot be exposed indefinitely to legal actions for allegedly defective products. Nevertheless, the ECJ still left scope for a UK court to allow substitution outside the 10-year period in certain factual circumstances.

Funding

It is important to understand how cases are funded as this has a bearing on the number, type and whether an action is brought in the first place. There are a number of ways to fund a personal injury case. These include:

- Conditional Fee Agreement, commonly known as a 'No Win No Fee' agreement.
- Legal Expenses Insurance – as part of household or car insurance a claimant may have legal expenses cover to help with legal costs. Legal Expense insurance is known as Before the Event Insurance (BTE).
- Trade Union – if the Claimant is a member of a trade union they may provide help with some legal issues.

If a claimant does not have legal expenses insurance or trade union help, their only option is to consider a 'No Win No Fee' agreement.

Conditional Fee Agreement

A Conditional Fee Agreement (CFA) is a 'no win no fee' agreement. It is a contract between the Claimant and his Solicitor which means that the Claimant does not pay the legal costs incurred if the matter is lost.

In the U.K the principle that the loser pays the winners costs partially stands. Thus, if the Claimant is successful the Defendant pays the Claimant's costs. If the Defendant is successful however, the claimant may not pay the Defendant's costs.

You may work for several years on cases without being paid. If you are unsuccessful with the case you will never be paid. Thus, you must carefully risk assess the cases you wish to take on. This assessment should also include an initial review of the medical notes and if still confident, a liability and causation report from a medical expert.

To account for the cases lost and the wait to be paid, the Solicitor is entitled to a 'success fee' which is an uplift in costs by a % to reflect risk. The Government changed the recoverability of legal costs and funding on 1 April 2013. These changes mean that the success fee and ATE insurance are not recoverable from the opponent. The Claimant thus pays the success fee from their compensation but limited to a maximum of 25% of the compensation.

The CFA aids access to justice. Few Claimants would be able to fund personal injury actions from their own private funds. There is a belief that acting under a CFA facilitates frivolous or fraudulent claims. This is untrue as the lack of recompense for a solicitors practice when acting in a case that is not successful acts as a counter measure to simply litigating anything. It makes little economic sense to work for nothing. Cases are therefore carefully chosen. Only those cases with a chance of success above 50% are pursued. This assessment is carefully reviewed at each stage. If it falls below 50% at any time, then the claimant is advised accordingly and usually the case comes to an end. Without supportive medical and technical evidence a claim is unlikely to be successful.

In short, if a claimant is successful:

- The opponent will pay the majority of the basic legal costs and disbursements (e.g. court fees and medical reports) subject to negotiation and assessment by the Court if no agreement is reached.

The opponent will not pay:

- The premium for the insurance policy to protect the Claimant against any risk of legal costs save for the part covering the expert report

- A 'success fee' which compensates the solicitor for the risk that the solicitor would not recover any legal fees if the claim was unsuccessful

If the Claimant loses the action:

- The Claimant is fully covered by the insurance policy for any disbursements

- The Solicitor writes off the costs incurred

- The insurance policy protects the Claimant from any of the opponent's legal costs (subject to Qualified One Way Costs Shifting and findings of fraud)

A Damages Based Agreement is an agreement whereby a solicitor and a client can agree to share the risk of litigation. Payment of solicitors' fees, counsel fees and VAT is dependent on achieving defined success criteria agreed when the DBA is entered into, and is based on a percentage of the sum recovered from the losing party/opponent.

To compensate for the risk of not being paid in the event of the case losing the DBA fee payable for solicitors' fees, counsel fees and VAT from monies recovered from the opponent will equate to a sum of up to 25% of general damages and pecuniary loss (other than future pecuniary loss) for a personal injury claim, and up to 50% of the sum recovered for all other matters (excluding employment claims). If there is an appeal there is no limit on the DBA percentage fee payable.

The DBA percentage fee for solicitor fees, counsel fees and VAT is paid by way of deduction from the sum recovered (damages) from the losing party. All other disbursements (including expert fees) and expenses are payable by the client in any event, and in addition to the DBA percentage fee.

Where a client obtains an entitlement to costs from an opponent, it will not be entitled to recover a fee directly based on the DBA percentage fee, but may be entitled to recover solicitors' fees based upon time spent and applicable hourly rates, plus all disbursements, reasonably and proportionately incurred and VAT if applicable. In any event, the receiving party cannot recover greater costs than incurred under the DBA.

However, it is worth noting that where a client enters into a DBA with a solicitor, there may potentially be an increase in irrecoverable costs from the opponent as a result of the indemnity principle, in particular where disputes are settled at an early stage.

Before the Event Legal Expenses Insurance

Before the Event legal expenses insurance is purchased with another policy of insurance such as car, household or a credit card. It funds the cost of legal advice and/or the costs of bringing or defending a court case. It is purchased in case a future legal action has to be fought or defended. Legal expenses insurance is *not* designed to pay the policy-holder the actual compensation that they are trying to recover through the court action. Nor does it cover someone's liability to pay compensation to others.

The legal expenses insurer will have a panel of legal firms which deal with a variety of actions covered by the policy. Some, but not all, policies cover clinical negligence cases. Few cover product liability claims. Thus, although a claimant may have legal expense insurance to pursue a claim, that insurance may prevent them from pursuing a manufacturer in say, an implant case. They would have to resort to a Conditional Fee Agreement as above. Cases that are pursued under legal expense insurance as also risk assessed to determine if there are prospects of success. Many of the legal firms on the insurance companies' panel will not have the necessary relevant experience of cosmetic surgery or product liability cases.

After the Event Insurance

After the Event Insurance (ATE Insurance) covers the legal costs and expenses involved in litigation. It is taken out when the Claimant has *already* decided to take a legal action and wants to insure against the risk of losing and having to pay some or all of the other side's costs. It will also cover the legal costs which a Claimant must pay when a claim is unsuccessful such as disbursements (medical report fees and court fees). It can also cover costs paid to the Defendant.

The overall concept of an ATE Insurance policy is that it will protect the claimant against costs risks right from the outset. Without such protection, few Claimant's would pursue a claim. Even for cases that are lost before trial the disbursements can run in to several thousands of pounds. To obtain such insurance, the insurers require that the prospects of being successful in the case must be above 50% and this is monitored regularly. Thus, if at any time the prospects of success in a case fall below 50%, the ATE insurance protection will be withdrawn and the case cannot proceed.

Under the Recovery of Costs Insurance Premiums in Clinical Negligence Proceedings (No2) Regulations 2013, it allows for part of the ATE premium to be recoverable from the Defendant. Reg. 3 states that the part of the premium which is recoverable 'shall not exceed that part of the premium which relates to the risk of incurring liability to pay for an expert report or reports relating to liability or causation in respect of clinical negligence in connection with the proceedings'. For further guidance on the recoverability of the premium see *Nokes v Heart of England Foundation Trust* [2015] EWHC B6.

The Path of a Claim

Disputes arising from cosmetic surgery are most frequently as a result of the informed consent process. Cosmetic surgeons are more than twice as likely as other specialist groups to face a claim, as a result of their surgery and failed informed consent. If the matter cannot be resolved by way of negotiation, then steps can be taken to commence legal proceedings.

The Civil Procedure Rules allow for flexibility and openness so that both sides can be constructive about resolving the dispute. Under the Pre-Action Protocol the Claimant Solicitor should request the disclosure of records (the records must be disclosed within 40 days of a request at the latest) and review the same. You should then instruct an appropriate expert to provide a liability and causation report. If this is a favourable report you can proceed to writing your Letter of Claim, drafting your client's witness statement, and obtaining the condition and prognosis report.

The Defendant insurers will investigate and obtain expert evidence. They will then provide a detailed response to your allegations of negligence within 4 months. Proceedings must not be commenced until after the expiry of the 4-month period. Consider this response carefully and check the records and expert reports again. It is prudent here to instruct Counsel if there is a denial of liability. Send the response to your expert and ask questions to try and flesh out whether there is a defence with merit. If liability is admitted, then further evidence can be gathered for losses and or treatment. If there is a denial of liability and matters are to proceed, then steps can be taken to commence legal proceedings.

The defendant insurers will ask the doctor to prepare a typed transcript of the relevant clinical entries indicating who wrote each entry (using initials for each staff member). They will also be obtaining a copy of any entries from relevant records such as the appointment diary etc. A copy of this will be sent to you as claimant solicitor. A factual account will be produced but this is not disclosable. It is for their use to understand how much the doctor recalls the events and what if any further evidence is needed.

Evidence

A well-researched and presented case will assist the court in making a determination. The following is a non-exhaustive list of considerations however it is dependent on the type of case and facts in issue.

- Research the best practice procedure for the treatment that the claimant has had and develop a list of documents you would expect to see.

- Check the regulatory issues pertaining to the clinic or hospital e.g. CQC reports.

- Establish the insurance coverage early.

- Read the standard terms and conditions given to the claimant. They usually restrict the liability of all involved. Don't assume that if the claimant paid the clinic that it is the clinic which is responsible for the services the claimant gets. Check the responsibility of the hospital, goods, doctors and anaesthetist.

- Is there anyone offering indemnity, if so seek a copy of the contract and review.

- Who carried out the operation – check that the surgeon performing the operation was the surgeon that the client saw from the start.

- Did the client see a representative or nurse at any point?

- How many times did the client see the surgeon to discuss the proposed surgery?

- Did the client have a cooling off period to think things through (it is usual to have at least 2 weeks).

- How many operations does the surgeon perform per year or how many procedures has the provider undertaken?

- Any deposit paid and how – how was the balance paid?

- GMC check out the doctor - Is he on the specialist register?

- Is he employed or independent?

- Check the qualifications of the surgeon – is he or she undertakingng surgery in the area of their expertise or trying something new?
- What was the outcome of the surgery that patient expected?
- What is the complication rate and re-operation rate generally and for that clinic? How does the surgeon measure their results? What was the client told? What proportion of patients need further corrective surgery?
- Alternatives to surgery include doing nothing – was the claimant advised of this?
- What are the potential risks and complications of surgery? What was the client told? Find out what the complications are, how often they occur and how they should be corrected. Was this communicated to the client?
- How was the client to measure the success of the procedure? Some clients have photographs of how they wish to look post-surgery and these are communicated to the surgeon. What was the outcome of those discussions? How was the client's expectation met?
- Was the need to repeat the procedure explained to the client? How many repeat procedures are needed to maintain the result (Botox or fillers).
- What about future surgeries, for example, implants need removing and replacing every 10 years or so?
- How would future cost be paid for?
- Was there an aftercare package?
- Who was the client to contact and how would they be looked after following surgery?

- If there were complications or problems, who was the client to see and who did she see, what was the outcome?

Pre-Action Matters

Whether a product liability claim or cosmetic surgery negligence matter, the parties to the dispute are required to act reasonably in exchanging information and documents in an attempt to settle their dispute without recourse to litigation. Sanctions may be imposed against parties who fail to comply with these requirement, for example, a party may be ordered to pay costs to the other party for failing to act reasonably. Follow the Pre-Action Protocol for the Resolution of Clinical Disputes if it is surgical or the Pre-Action Protocol for Personal Injury if not. The Protocol for Clinical Disputes is intended to apply to all claims against hospitals, GPs, dentists and other healthcare providers (both NHS and private) which involve an injury that is alleged to be the result of clinical negligence. The Protocol provides for a defendant to be given four months to investigate and respond to a Letter of Claim before proceedings are served. If this is not possible, the claimant's solicitor should give as much notice of the intention to issue proceedings as is practicable. This Protocol does not alter the statutory time limits for starting court proceedings. If a claim is issued after the relevant statutory limitation period has expired, the defendant will be entitled to use that as a defence to the claim. If proceedings are started to comply with the statutory time limit before the parties have followed the procedures in this Protocol, the parties should apply to the court for a stay of the proceedings while they so comply.

The Protocol for Personal Injury actions is primarily designed for personal injury claims which are likely to be allocated to the fast track and to the entirety of those claims: not only to the personal injury element of a claim which also includes, for instance, property damage.

Medical records, medical reports and a detailed Letter of Claim must be sent to the Defendant by the Claimant (ideally before proceedings are commenced). This sets out the basis for the claim and the evidence in support. The Defendant then writes a letter of response either admitting liability or setting out the reasons for a denial. The Defendant is able to obtain their own medical evidence.

Court Fee Payments

For cases where a court fee is required, the court is able to review the client's financial circumstances and apply a fee remission. Ideally, clients should be asked whether they are eligible for fee exemption before proceedings are issued but if you are just coming to this now you can apply to refund fees paid. The form EX160 is self-explanatory and should be completed with as much detail as is available before being sent to the client to finalise in order to increase a timely response from clients. They need to include details of their income as those in low income, little to no savings or on certain benefits may qualify for fee remission. If they are in receipt of one of the following state benefits they are exempt, such as:

- Income based Jobseekers Allowance (JSA)
- Income related Employment and Support Allowance (ESA)
- Income Support
- Universal Credit (and earning less than £6,000 per year)
- State Pension (Guarantee Credit)

The client needs to have less than £3,000 in savings and investments if under 61. They can have up to £16,000 in savings if their fee is between £1,000 and £10,000, or if they or their partner are 61 and over. If they are not on any of those benefits, they need to earn less than £1,085 a month before tax if they are single, or £1,245 if they have a partner. They can earn an extra £245 on top of that for each child they have. For example, if your client has a partner and 2 children they have to earn less than £1,735 to be eligible for help with court fees.

The EX160 form can only be completed and signed by the client up to a month or so before the remission is requested. There is a strict three-month deadline which applies to backdated payments. It is important to determine the client's position as not only will it save your firm from having to pay the sum or the client, but Defendants are asking what investigations were made before they will agree disbursements. If your client could have received a fee remission then you may find a challenge to recover the said fees from the Defendant.

Issuing Proceedings and Court Documents

Proceedings begin when the claimant issues a *claim form* that must contain or be accompanied by the *particulars of claim* (Part 7 Civil Procedure Rules). The claim form and particulars of claim must set out a summary of the basic facts of the claim against the defendant as the Letter of Claim did. Failing to do this may allow the defendant to strike out the claim. You need to be certain therefore of all the issues and causes of action upon which you will be relying.

The claimant will have to pay a fee to issue the claim form, the amount of which depends on the value and nature of the claim. Court fees are expensive. The Claimant may get a fee remission as discussed earlier. The documents have to be served on the defendant in accordance with Part 6 Civil Procedure Rules and within prescribed timeframes. When the defendant is served with court proceedings, he has to indicate whether he accepts or intends to defend the claim (Part 10 Civil Procedure Rules). Again, this must be done within the prescribed time limits and the court must be notified. If the defendant wishes to defend the claim he must serve a defence, including any counterclaim, normally within 28 days of receiving the claim form (Part 15 Civil Procedure Rules). This defence is also an important document because if it is regarded as weak, the claimant can seek to strike it out or seek summary judgment against the defendant. A failure to serve a defence will allow the claimant to win the case by default.

Further court documents may be served and filed at court in order to clarify each party's position. All court documents have to be accompanied by a *statement of truth* verifying the truth of the information contained in the document. Court documents including the claim form, particulars of claim, defence and any counterclaim will, in certain circumstances, be accessible to third parties.

Case Management

All cases are actively managed by the courts to ensure that they proceed properly. The courts will consider whether the likely benefits of taking a particular step will justify the cost. Case management also allows the court to try to encourage the parties to settle their disputes without the need for trial, through alternative dispute resolution procedures (ADR) such as mediation. The court will also order budgets in cases over £25,000. Costs and budgets are beyond the scope of this book but suffice to say that you need to think clearly about what expert evidence you will need, when counsel will be asked to contribute and get quotes from all for inclusion and agreement within the budget.

Disclosure of Documents

A party must disclose to the other party the documents (including electronic documents, (for example, e-mails) it seeks to rely on, as well as the documents which adversely affect its own or another party's case or support another party's case. This may include confidential documents if they are relevant to the dispute. Certain documents may be exempt from disclosure on the grounds of 'legal professional privilege'. Medical errors are rarely caused by bad individuals, more often it is the result of bad systems. Understanding what should happen when things go wrong means that you can ask for the supporting documentation. If there is a lack of documentation, then you are in a strong position to seek a settlement.

If something goes wrong, the doctor should (and you should check that they have and ask disclosure of the relevant documents):

- Review the patient's clinical care – without clear notes it is easy to forget the details.

- Report the incident to the organisation or clinic – it helps the clinic to learn how to reduce risk and improve patient safety. What procedures do they have in place?

- Contact the medical defence organisation.

- Complete an adverse reporting form.
- Apologise to the patient and be open – it is not an admission of liability to apologise when something has gone wrong with the patient's treatment and is the right thing to do.
- Familiarise themselves with the complaints procedure of the clinic/hospital.
- Document details of the incident as soon as possible after it happens – document the time and date of the incident, report of error, location, description of the incident, immediate action taken, severity of injury or complaint, presumed cause or circumstances.

Other documents and policies to ask for depending on the type of adverse event:

- What is the prescribing practice (for drug related errors)? What failsafe in the prescribing system have they introduced so that a clinician cannot prescribe a larger than recommended dose of a drug without overriding a warning system? What risk management tools do they use in relation to prescribing?
- The reporting policies for when an adverse incident has occurred to the clinic, hospital and insurers. How do they deal with mistakes and put systems in place to make sure they don't happen again?
- The WHO Surgical Safety Checklist for Patient Safety.
- All medical and operating notes.
- All correspondence passing between the clinic, surgeon and patient.
- Contracts.
- Copies of payments.

- Root cause analysis of an incident.
- Risk assessments.
- Qualifications and expertise of doctor.
- Ask how often the procedure has been performed by the practitioner and how often they encounter complications and what they are.
- Aftercare documentation and advice.
- The full cost of the procedure in writing.

Witness Statements

If a party wants to provide oral evidence at trial, then it should disclose this evidence in written format. This can be a vital stage in the proceedings as what is said in a witness statement may be determine whether party seeks to settle the dispute. The statement should 'tell the story' in chronological order and should include all factual issues in the case. It should be written in plain English and clear language. The statement is a statement of fact, not opinion. Above all things, the witness statement must be true and certified to be so and signed. Electronic signatures are now allowed.

Statements are exchanged several weeks before the trial and this allows a period of reflection in order to consider the issues and formulate any offers. Witnesses will be cross-examined at trial. The case of *Wilson v Lassman* [2017] EWHC 85 (Ch) contained guidance on obtaining witness evidence. It highlighted the need for taking a careful record of the way in which the witness statement is taken, not just the content of the statement. Recording the conversation, amendments to questionnaires and discussions pertaining to those amendments are important.

All statements are signed by a 'statement of truth' which is a statement signed by a party to verify that the contents of the document referred to are true. It will usually appear at the end of the document being verified. Attention is drawn to the consequences of signing a false statement of truth. The statement of truth should be in the following form:

'[I believe]/[the [Claimant/Defendant] believes] that the facts stated in this [witness statement are true' (Part 22 Civil Procedure Rules).'

If any statement of case is not verified by a statement of truth, the statement of case will remain effective unless it is struck out by an Order of the Court. However, a party may not rely on the contents of a statement of case as evidence until it has been verified by a statement of truth. If a witness statement is not signed with a statement of truth, the Court may direct that it shall not be admissible as evidence. In certain circumstances, a false statement made in a document verified by a statement of truth may lead to liability for contempt of Court. Proceedings for contempt of Court may be brought against a person if he makes, or causes to be made, a false statement without an honest belief in its truth. Contempt of Court may be punishable by a fine and/or imprisonment and/or the sequestration of assets.

Expert Evidence

If a party needs to rely on the opinion of an expert on a particular issue, the court's permission will be needed if not already obtained before commencement of proceedings. An expert witness must be independent, with an overriding duty to the court rather than the instructing party. The court can order the parties to share the evidence of an expert on a particular issue pursuant to Part 35 Civil Procedure Rules. There can be more than one expert witness per case if there are several areas of expertise to address. An expert witness may be involved in court proceedings and may be called to give evidence although there are strict rules about the content and format of an expert witness's report and the evidence he may give.

In cosmetic surgery claims the expert evidence will be a liability and causation report, opinion and prognosis report and medical records. There may also be engineering evidence to examine a product which is allegedly defective.

A cosmetic surgeon expert witness should be qualified by his or her knowledge or experience to give an opinion on a particular issue(s) to a court. The notion of expert evidence requires that there be matters at issue which require expertise for their observation, analysis or description. Expert evidence is sought in relation to any factual issue in dispute:

- Where there is an acknowledged "body of expertise" that is governed by established principles and rules of conduct;
- Which is pertinent to an issue to be decided by the court; and
- Which is outside the experience of the judge.

To be of assistance to a court the expert must not only give an opinion but support it, and show the court that it is well founded. Expert evidence will often include:

- opinions based on the facts adduced in the case:
- factual evidence obtained by the witness which requires expertise in its interpretation and presentation;
- explanations of technical terms or topics;
- evidence of a specialist nature;
- reference to relevant publications and literature. All material or literature relied upon should be served either with the report or in sufficient time before trial to be reviewed by any other experts and by the trial judge. Permission will be required from the Court before additional material can be adduced at trial.

Trial

The trial will be determined by the judge alone. English trials are predominantly oral, requiring each party's counsel to make oral submissions and draw the judge's attention to the relevant evidence and law.

However, before the start of the trial, the judge will generally have read the court documents, witness statements, experts' reports and skeleton arguments drafted by counsel. The judge does not make his own investigations, but he may put questions to counsel or witnesses.

In summary, the trial consists of each party's advocate setting out their case and calling on the evidence of the witnesses and experts that they seek to rely on. These witnesses may be cross-examined by the opposing barrister. The trial will end with both parties' barristers summing up the evidence and making submissions on the relevant law. The judge will make his decision based on the evidence and arguments put before him. Judgment may be given immediately after the trial or, in more complicated cases, reserved until a later date when the judge has reflected on the issues. If a party seeks to appeal the judgement it must obtain the permission of the court. Permission will only be given in limited circumstances.

Winning a case at trial requires careful preparation. Have a clear plan that includes a list of all points that need to be proved and the evidence that will be required to prove them. While agreed statements of fact can simplify matters, it is likely that there are several factual issues that will be very much disputed, and will require formal proof at trial.

Restoring a Company

If a Company is struck off it means that it has been removed from the Companies Register at Companies House. This means that it has ceased to exist, and all of the Company's assets will become bona vacanti. If a company is no longer trading it may be necessary to restore it to the register in order to commence legal proceedings.

Firstly, contact the court to find out current handling times as soon as you are aware that you will need to commence. You need to leave yourself with enough time to carry out the necessary steps. You may need to make an application to extend time for service pursuant to CPR 7.6 (even if an insurer agrees) to facilitate the restoration of the company. It is a good idea to get insurers agreement in principle and to append that to the application.

Any company which is restored to the register is deemed to have continued in existence. The registrar can restore a company if he receives a court order. There are no time limits for applying for personal injury claims. If you are restoring a company registered in England or Wales, you must apply to the Court by completing a Part 8 Claim form (N208). The Registrar of companies usually hears restoration cases in chambers once a week on Friday afternoon. Cases are also heard at district registries or you can make an application to a county court that has authority to wind up the company. You must give the registrar at least 10 days notice of the hearing.

You must serve the claim form, witness statements and supporting evidence on the appropriate register of companies and the solicitor dealing with any 'bona vacantia' assets. You serve on the Treasury Solicitor unless the company's registered office is in Lancashire or Cornwall, when it should be served on the solicitor to the Duchy of Lancaster or Cornwall. Documents can be delivered by post but recorded delivery is safer.

Registrar of Companies (England and Wales)
Companies House
Crown Way
Cardiff
CF14 3UZ
DX 33050 Cardiff
Telephone 0303 1234500

You will need to send to the court:

- Evidence that the originating document was served.
- Written confirmation that there is no objection to the restoration of the company from the solicitor dealing with the bona vacantia assets.
- Details about when the company was incorporated and the natures of its objects – attach a copy of the certificate of incorporation, the memorandum of association and articles of association.

- The membership, officers and directors and secretary of the company.
- Trading activity e.g. When it stopped trading.
- Explanation of any failure to deliver accounts or returns or notices.
- Details of the striking off and dissolution .
- Other information explaining the reason for the application.
- Witness statement detailing who is seeking the restoration and why.
- Address of registered office of the company.
- Share capital of the company.

When the Order is made the applicant must deliver a copy of the court Order with the court seal to the Registrar to restore the company. A company is restored when you deliver the order to the Registrar. A notice will be placed in the relevant Gazette. The Gazette is the official newspaper record in the United Kingdom. There are 3 of them:

- the London Gazette, for companies incorporated in England and Wales;
- the Edinburgh Gazette, for companies incorporated in Scotland; and
- the Belfast Gazette, for companies incorporated in Northern Ireland.

When the Registrar of Companies publishes a notice to strike off or restore a company, the notice will appear in the Gazette for the part of the United Kingdom in which the company was formed. These Gazettes are published weekly and can be found at:

http://www.gazettes-online.co.uk

Group Litigation Orders

A Group Litigation Order would be made if there were a number of litigants suing a manufacturer for defective product under the Consumer Protection Act. This is to ensure that the litigant's cases are case managed together pursuant to Part 19 CPR. A Group Litigation would take place in the High Court. The High Court has jurisdiction over most matters through its District Registries and the Royal Courts of Justice in London. It is divided into three divisions: Chancery, Queen's Bench and Family. The Chancery Division deals with companies generally and such specialist matters as wills, trusts, insolvency and tax. The Queen's Bench Division (QBD) deals with all other civil matters including contractual disputes, personal injury cases, industrial accidents, defamation cases and negligence claims. A Group Litigation is dealt with in the QBD. The Court of Appeal deals with appeals from a decision of a High Court judge. On issues of public importance there is a further and final stage of appeal, to the Supreme Court, where the appeal is heard usually by five Justices. Occasionally, matters may be referred to the European Court of Justice for guidance on points of EU law.

Judges play an active role in managing civil cases once they have started (especially in large or complex cases and GLO matters), helping to ensure they proceed as quickly and efficiently as possible. This includes:

- encouraging the parties to co-operate with each other in the conduct of the case;
- helping the parties to settle the case;

- encouraging the parties to use an alternative dispute resolution procedure if appropriate; and

- controlling the progress of the case.

The judge ensures that all parties involved are given the opportunity to have their case presented and considered as fully and fairly as possible. During the case the judge will ask questions on any point he or she feels needs clarification. The judge also decides on all matters of procedure which may arise during a hearing.

By joining forces claimants can split the costs between them, increase the availability of similar evidence and the sharing of knowledge and litigation risk. An application for a GLO may be made at any time before or after any relevant claims have been issued and may be made either by a claimant or a defendant. If the application is successful the Court will manage all claims covered by the order in a coordinated way. Under CPR 19.11, a GLO will establish a group register in which the relevant claims will be entered, specify the GLO issues that will identify the claims to be managed as a group, and specify which court will manage those claims. All judgments, orders and directions of the court will be binding on all claims within the GLO unless ordered otherwise.

There is no definitive procedure in place whereby solicitors and claimants are adequately able to locate others who may have claims which give rise to common or related issues of fact or law. You can search the court database for cases currently filed but yet to be determined. You may search cases by party name and division however the database provides limited information as to the subject matter of proceedings and may produce hundreds, if not thousands of individual cases currently before the courts. When a GLO is approved by the court it is common to order the parties to publicise its existence so that all relevant claims can be managed within it. A copy of the order should also be supplied to the Law Society. Solicitors acting for GLO claimants are encouraged to contact the Law Society Multi Party Action Information Service. A list of GLO's is also maintained on the justice website which also includes details of the lead solicitors and case issues defined by the GLO. The Law Society often assists in putting a claimant in touch with other parties who may also be interested in applying for a Group Litigation Order in their case.

Group actions carry risk for any claimant. If they lose their case they risk an adverse costs order which can cause a reduction in full costs and damages recovery (as an offset for any generic costs reduction) for every other claimant on the GLO. The more defendants the greater the risk and care must be taken when putting claimants onto the register. Every case added increases the risk of incomplete recovery of damages and costs. Any cases added must have ATE or BTE insurance that provides adequate cover not only for the claimant's personal liability to the Defendant, but also for shared adverse costs orders and costs sharing in relation to the generic aspects of the GLO. Adverse cost cover is usually for a minimum of £10,000.

The Poly Implant Prothese (PIP) breast implant scandal saw 47,000 British women affected. About 300,000 women in 65 countries are believed to have received PIP implants. Europe was a major market, but more than half went to South America. Private clinics fitted 95% of the implants the other 5% were performed by the NHS mostly for breast reconstruction following cancer. All the women were fitted with silicone implants containing industrial grade chemicals never intended for medical use. The company that made the silicone went out of business. Claimants sued the cosmetic surgery clinics where they were fitted with their implants. Most of the clinics went out of business. Few had adequate or any insurance to cover an action under the Consumer Protection Act. Many Claimants were left without compensation.

Costs

If the Claimant is successful in the action she is awarded her legal costs in addition to compensation for injury and losses. Arguments regarding cost issues can result in a lower award. A cost award for a GLO will involve generic costs generated by the lead firms on common issues as well as individual firm's costs. The larger the number of Claimants and the longer the case proceeds then the greater the costs. All cases above £25,000 now require a cost budget to be filed setting out the expected cost of the litigation to trial.

It is usual for costs to be negotiated separately and if no agreement can be reached, a further court assessment will take place. In "part-payment" for the loss of recoverability of the CFA success fee from the Defendant, Lord Justice Jackson gave Claimants a 10% uplift on general damages (injury compensation). In part-payment for the loss of the right to recover the after-the-event insurance premium from a losing Defendant, Lord Justice Jackson gave Claimants the protection of "qualified one way costs shifting", known as QOCS or QOWCS (pronounced "kw-ocs"). The basic principle is that an unsuccessful Claimant will not be liable for Defendant's costs save where the claimant has failed to obtain a judgment more advantageous than a defendant's Part 36 offer (i.e. an offer to settle). This is "one-way costs shifting". QOCS applies only to personal injury actions.

QOCS does not apply to a pre-action application for disclosure which is often made to obtain documents from a Defendant pre-issue in order to determine if the case is worth pursuing. In short, if a Claimant loses on liability QOCS effectively allows the Claimant to walk away from the failed claim, because there is no award for 'damages and interest' against which the costs order can bite. Likewise the Claimant who discontinues an action.

Overall, Claimants are at less risk in pursuing cases when not facing a cost award if the case is lost. A successful Defendant however, will pay their solicitors costs without the ability to recover them from the Claimant. A Defendant has only 2 options for cost recovery from the Claimant: Part 36 offers which are not beaten or demonstrating 'fundamental dishonesty'.

Part 36 offers are an offer to settle within a specified time. If the Claimant fails to accept the offer and further fails to exceed the offer at trial, the Defendant is entitled to seek payment of their costs from the last day for acceptance of the offer to trial. Part 36 is a stand-alone provision. Offers need to be calculated to put the Claimant at risk.

Orders for costs made against the claimant may be enforced where the claim is found on the balance of probabilities to be fundamentally dishonest. What is fundamentally dishonest? It entails straightforward fraud but also a lower level of dishonesty than fraud. Where there has been a genuine accident justifying an award of damages but where the Claimant has presented fabricated or exaggerated losses the "fundamental" element introduces weighing scales. Where a minor bit of padding of losses or injury may not generate loss of QOCS, it's where the edifice of exaggeration is so great 'the majority of the Claimant's case collapses'. The Defendant is entitled to cost recovery but not the full extent of the costs incurred.

Fundamental dishonesty is a hot topic that likely to dominate the next 2-3 years as cases filter through.

Enforcement of Judgement

When a judgment is obtained, the unsuccessful party may make the payment voluntarily. If it does not, various enforcement procedures are available. There are various ways to enforce a Judgment and at this stage, the appropriate method depends on the debtor's circumstances.

Charging Order – If the Defendant owns or has an interest in a property, it is possible to secure the Judgment against the property. Although the charge does not guarantee immediate payment, it does secure the debt and interest accrues at 8% per annum. It is usually worth getting a Charge on a property if there is equity in the property.

Order for sale – Once you have a Charging Order you can enforce it by an application to sell the property.

County Court Bailiff / High Court Enforcement Officer – A County Court Bailiff or High Court Enforcement Officer will attend at the Defendant's premises and collect the money due, or take steps to enforce payment by seizing and selling goods, or will report back as to the Defendant's assets. Entry can be forced into commercial premises e.g. by employing a locksmith to pick the lock but entry **cannot** be forced into residential premises. The items seized must generally be sold by auction. The costs of instructing Bailiff/HCEO are partly recoverable from the debtor if the debt is collected in full. If the bailiff does not recover the debt, the costs are payable by the claimant solicitor.

Attachment of Earnings Order – When a defendant is working, this is often an appropriate method of enforcement. You will need to know the name and address of his/her employer. The debt is paid out of the defendant's salary by the employer.

Third Party Debt Order – A Third Party Debt Order is usually made to stop the Defendant taking money out of his or her bank or building society account. The money owed is paid directly to the Claimant or Claimant's solicitor by the debtor's Bank/Building Society from their account. A Third Party Debt Order can also be made against anyone who owes the Defendant money

Information Order – If the defendant is attempting to avoid enforcement, you can apply to the court for an order that they attend before a court officer to answer questions with regard to their assets and means.

Insolvency – If Judgment remains unsatisfied the option of insolvency exists if the debt is for an amount over £750.

CHAPTER FIVE
PRODUCT LIABILITY UNDER THE CONSUMER PROTECTION ACT

When a business supplies products to consumers, they need to make sure the products are safe e.g. implants. Product liability is the area of law in which manufacturers, distributors, suppliers and retailers are held responsible for any injuries products cause. Regardless of any contractual limitations of liability, if a product or any of its component parts are defective, its manufacturer may be liable for damage under the Consumer Protection Act (CPA) or the common law of negligence. An action under the CPA or for negligence can be brought for death, personal injury and damage caused to private property as the result of a product defect. Neither type of action can be used to compensate for pure economic or consequential loss. It is therefore important that manufacturers retain and invest in:

- Pre – market safety data included in the manufacturer's technical file including toxicity data, clinical and preclinical data, risk assessment and quality systems.

- Post – market safety data including information about the safety and performance of the device gathered about the device in use. Some of this post –market safety data will meet the criteria for vigilance and will need to be reported to the competent authority.

The CPA introduced statutory liability for defective products. Liability under the CPA exists alongside liability in negligence, and in some cases a common law claim may succeed where a claim would not be available under the CPA. The CPA imposes strict liability on manufacturers of defective products for harm caused by those products. This means that people who are injured by defective products can sue for compensation without having to prove that the manufacturer was negligent. It is merely necessary to prove that the product was defective, and that any injury was most likely caused by the product.

Applicability

A claim may be brought under the CPA by any person who is injured by a 'defective product', regardless of whether that person purchased the product. A claim may be brought for death, personal injury or damage to private property in excess of £275. The Act imposes no financial limit on the producer's total liability.

Who Is Liable?

Under the CPA, the 'producer' of a product is liable for any defects. The producer is the manufacturer of the finished product or of a component of the finished product, or any person responsible for an industrial or other process to which any essential characteristic of the product is attributable. Liability may also be imposed on any party who holds itself out to be the producer through the use of a name or trade mark, and any person who imported the product into the European Community. As such, there may be more than one party liable under the CPA in respect of the same damage. Liability is joint and several, so the injured party may sue any or all of these people. Liability cannot be excluded or limited. The main responsibility is to ensure that products are safe by:

- warning consumers about potential risks;
- providing information to help consumers understand the risks;
- monitoring the safety of products;
- taking action if a safety problem is found.

Manufacturers need to take an active approach to preventing safety problems, otherwise they risk being sued, fined or imprisoned. Particular care should be taken with high-risk products such as medicines.

What Is a 'Defective Product'?

A 'product' can include goods, electricity and the component parts of any product. Where a component of or raw material incorporated into a finished product is defective both the manufacturer of the component and the manufacturer of the finished product are potentially liable. A product is defective for the purposes of the CPA if its safety, including not only the risk of personal injury but also the risk of damage to property, is "not such as persons generally are entitled to expect". A product will not generally be considered defective just because a safer version is later put on the market. In assessing the safety of the product the court will take into account all of the circumstances, specifically including:

- all aspects of the marketing of the product;
- the use of any mark in relation to the product;
- instructions and warnings;
- what might reasonably be expected to be done with the product at the time the product was supplied.

This last factor allows the court to take account of the 'state of the art' at the time of supply. The case of *Wilkes v DePuy* (2016) EWHC 3096 (QB) has provided a landmark judgment on the meaning of "defect" under the Consumer Protection Act 1987 ("the Act"). Mr Justice Hickinbottom sitting in the High Court adopted an objective test for safety by reference to what the public at large are *entitled* to expect of the product. It was a departure from the approach taken in *A v National Blood Authority* ("*A v NBA*") [2001] 3 All ER 289.

The Act which implements EC Council Directive 85/374/EEC ("the Directive") applies to virtually all products supplied to consumers yet there is very little guidance in the Directive on the meaning of "defect". It was thought preferable to leave it open to allow case law to develop. We now have such clarity.

The case involved the claimant's metal on metal left hip replacement comprising of a steel femoral shaft called a "C-Stem" which fit into the hollow of the thigh bone connected to a prosthetic femoral head by way of a taper sleeve adapter. Three years after insertion, the Claimant felt his left hip "give way" and the stem had fractured, necessitating replacement with a different model. The Claimant claimed under the Act against the Defendant and in negligence. Mr Justice Hickinbottom heard the trial of a preliminary issue of whether the Defendant was liable to the Claimant pursuant to section 3 of the Act.

The Act provides under section 3 that there is a "defect" in a product if the safety of the product is "not such as persons generally are entitled to expect", taking into account "all the circumstances", including:

- the manner and purposes for which the product had been marketed, and any instructions given;
- what might reasonably be expected to be done with the product; and
- the time the producer first put the product into circulation.

If damage is caused wholly or partly by the defect, the producer of the product shall be liable for the damage. The Court looked at *Ide v ATB Sales Limited* (2008) EWCA Civ 414 which stated that 'a claimant must prove a causal link between the defect and the damage, but is not required to prove the cause of the lack of safety or why the product failed'. The judge stated that the test for the appropriate level of "safety" required 'an objective approach confirming that safety "is inherently and necessarily a relative concept" and that "no medicinal product, if effective, can be absolutely safe"'. The potential benefits (including utility) of such products therefore have to be balanced against their risks. He considered that 'apart from the three specific matters set out in section 3 of the Act that must be taken into account', the court must maintain a 'flexible and holistic approach to the assessment of the appropriate level of safety, including which circumstances are relevant and the weight to be given to each in each case'.

Thus the judge concluded that the "avoidability" of the defect should be considered within the context of the risk-benefit balance of the product itself, without 'unduly focussing on the acts/omissions of the designer/producer'. In some cases, the ease and extent to which a risk could be eliminated or mitigated (including cost) may bear upon the level of safety that the public generally is entitled to expect. However, for a medical product like a prosthesis, he thought that a 'detailed consideration of whether a particular risk was or was not "avoidable" would be unlikely to be fruitful'. It was a matter of degree: 'it was not suggested that the stem should not have failed at all; rather it failed earlier than it should have done'.

The court also considered compliance with mandatory standards and regulations. He found that 'compliance would not provide a complete defence but would carry considerable weight and in appropriate cases provide "powerful evidence" that the level of safety required by the Act had been satisfied'. This is particularly the case when 'all aspects of the product's design, manufacture and marketing has been the subject of substantial scrutiny by a regulatory body comprised of individuals selected for their experience and expertise'.

This case differs from *A v NBA*. Previously, the first step was to "identify the harmful characteristic which caused the injury". The judge thought this approach circular: 'proof of a connection between defect and damage cannot rationally be attempted without ascertainment of whether there is a defect, and if so, what the defect might be'. Concentrating on causation at the outset was "a distraction from the true focus of the Directive and the Act, which is on defect". A test of what persons generally are entitled to expect does not require further description.

In *A v NBA* the court classified "standard" (a product which performs as the producer intends) and "non-standard" products (a product which is different, deficient or inferior in terms of safety from the standard product and where the harmful characteristic causes the damage). He excluded the 'relevance of risk-benefit in the case of a non-standard product'. Mr Justice Hickinbottom thought this classification was 'positively unhelpful and potentially dangerous' and a 'distraction from the exercise the court was required to undertake, namely consideration of the appropriate level of safety taking into account all relevant circumstances'.

The marketing of a product is one of the three specific matters set out in section 3 of the Act. There was no obligation on the producer to provide any information directly to the patient, who was assisted by his surgeon. Mr Justice Hickinbottom stated that it was "unarguable" that it was a relevant circumstance where a learned intermediary (who has his general professional knowledge but also the manufacturer's Instructions for Use ("IFU") – including warnings) has chosen a particular prosthesis for a particular patient, particularly where there is no obligation on the producer to provide information directly to the patient.

The judge held that the C-Stem did not suffer from a defect. The product complied with relevant mandatory standards and regulatory requirements. The IFU were regulator approved and warned of severe loading placing the patient at higher risk of hip replacement failure in cases of obesity, manual labour, participation in active sport and high activity levels. The fatigue failure of the Claimant's C-Stem was "rare, unpredicted and unpredictable" and was a risk expressly warned of in the IFU as one of the most frequently encountered adverse events and complications.

Whilst this case assists manufacturers of high regulatory thresholds and standards it is unclear in relation to causation what must be proved where the Claimant's case was based upon a defect causing an increased risk of injury or damage. Having found no defect, the judge did not need to consider causation. The judgment helps to determine what constitutes a defect under the Act. However, each case must be viewed on its own merits.

Defences to a Claim Under the CPA

If a manufacturer believes that the problem with the implant was caused by a fault in the production process, they can enter a claims handling agreement whereby they agree to settle claims provided they meet certain criteria, without an admission of liability. The Claimant is expected to enter into a confidentiality agreement as part of the settlement.

Although liability under the CPA is strict, a manufacturer has a number of defences available if a claim is made. It is a defence to show:

- the injured person has been unable to discharge the burden of proof;
- the defendant is able to establish one of the statutory defences in s 4 of the Act;
- the claimant is debarred from proceeding by one or more of the Act's time limits;
- the defences of contributory negligence or volenti non fit injuria (the willing acceptance of risk).

Statutory defences:

- that the product is defective in order to comply with domestic or European law i.e. an inevitable fault of obeying other laws;
- the production of evidence that the manufacturer did not supply the product (e.g. It is a copy of their product);
- that the product was not manufactured or supplied in the course of a business or with a view to profit;
- that the defect did not exist at the time the product was put into circulation. The manufacturer would have to show that they could not reasonably be expected to discover the safety fault. For instance, where a defective prosthesis was used in a hip operation, the court was required to consider when the defect had arisen. It was held that if there had been a defect, it would have been identified at or before final inspection. The product was therefore not defective at the time of its supply.

- The development risks defence – This statutory defence will succeed if the producer of the product can prove that it could not have been expected to have discovered the defect while the product was in its control because of the state of scientific and technical knowledge at that time. For instance, in the blood transfusion case, the development risks defence was raised. The court found that, at the time of the transfusions, no screening test was available and therefore the risk of supplying a defective blood product was unavoidable. It held that the development risks defence was not available where it was known that a particular product could have harmful consequences. The case highlights the limited scope of the development risks defence.
- if the party is being sued because it manufactured a component – that the defect is a defect within the finished product, and came about because of the way the finished product was designed or because of instructions given by the manufacturer of the finished product.

The 'development risks' defence creates a defence if the "scientific and technical knowledge" at the time the product was manufactured could be particularly important in relation to innovative and high-tech products. However, it has been argued that the wording of the UK law is less strict than the wording of the law at European level, which deals with the state of scientific and technical knowledge generally rather than what a producer of similar products might be expected to discover.

How Long Are Producers Liable for?

The basic limitation period for claims under the CPA is three years from the date of damage or injury. However, since damage may not be immediately apparent, an alternative period of three years from the date when the claimant knew – or could reasonably have known – of the claim, is provided. Since a product may remain in circulation for many years, a claim cannot be made more than ten years after the product was put into circulation.

The issue with implants is that they generally have a life expectancy of around 10 years before needing to be removed and replaced. If a claimant has had her implants for 10 years and has no rupture, then the defence will be her implants needed to be replaced at around the same period. Consequently, the claimant will have suffered no loss unless the implants had ruptured. If the claimant has already had her implants replaced then she will not be seeking a remedy for replacement but will be seeking damages on the grounds of disappointment, the cost of surgery and any injury caused and/or for undergoing a procedure that would not have taken place on the balance of probability at time that it did. This is a question of fact determined on the balance of probability. If she can prove that 'fact' then she recovers damages appropriate to when it is probable or possible that she would have had the surgery anyway. If the implants were replaced at no cost by the clinic and did not rupture early, there is a real risk that the court will consider that she would have had the implants replaced by that date and therefore she is entitled to disappointment damages only. These are unlikely to be substantial enough to warrant bringing a claim.

If the clinic has agreed to undertake removal and replacement surgery at no cost it is usual for them to ask the Claimant to complete a waiver or discharge form before agreeing to undertake the surgery. Under the Unfair Contract Terms Act a defendant is precluded from being able to avoid its liability for future personal injury losses arising from the remedial surgery but it may bind the claimant for the original surgery. The Claimant needs to have had sufficient time to consider it. It would be worth obtaining Counsels opinion on the waiver if action was sought.

Common Law Negligence

A claim may be brought in negligence as well as a breach in statutory duty. They are usually pleaded together but can be separate. There is a three-stage test for establishing a duty of care and how to apply it. For a claimant to succeed in proving her claim in common law negligence she must first prove that a duty of care was owed by the defendant manufacturer. In deciding whether the defendant owes a duty of care the court adopts a three-stage test:

1) Is there a relationship of proximity between the parties?

2) Was the injury to the claimant foreseeable?

3) Is it fair, just and reasonable to impose a duty?

Was There a Relationship of Proximity?

The principle of 'duty of care' was established by *Donoghue v Stevenson* (1932) when Lord Atkin identified that there was a general duty to take reasonable care to avoid *foreseeable* injury to a 'neighbour'. Proximity is the shorthand for the neighbour test. A neighbour is defined as 'someone who may be reasonably contemplated as closely and directly affected by an act'.

Once the court has determined that a common law duty of care exists between the parties, the claimant must prove that the duty has been breached. Breach of duty in negligence liability may be found to exist where the defendant fails to meet the standard of care required by law. The test of breach of duty is generally objective, however, there may be slight variations to this.

Was Injury Foreseeable?

The Claimant must satisfy the test of foreseeability, type of damage versus how it occurred, and type of and severity of the damage—the 'egg-shell skull' rule. Even if the defendant caused the damage they will not necessarily be liable for everything that can be traced back to the original wrongdoing. The defendant is liable for damage only if it was the foreseeable consequence of the breach of duty. It is not necessary to show that the defendant should have foreseen precisely what happened. It is enough if the injury is of a type that could have been foreseen even if it came about in an unexpected way. Compensation is paid in order to return the patient to the position they would theoretically have been in had the harm not occurred. A monetary value will attach not just to actual expenses incurred but to the loss of amenity experienced and the pain and suffering endured in consequence of the injury. The theory is that this promotes accountability and ensures that those at fault are deterred from future acts of carelessness by the need to pay compensation. Although somewhat lessened by indemnity from an insurer, there is the emotional deterrent and insurance premium increases which can act as a measure.

Is It Fair and Reasonable?

Whether or not a duty of care exists it is necessary to consider whether it is just and reasonable to impose a duty. This can be very broad as can be seen from *Hedley Byrne and Co. Ltd v Heller and Partners Ltd* [1964] when Lord Pearce stated:

> *"How wide the sphere of the duty of care in negligence is to be laid depends ultimately upon the courts' assessment of the demands of society for protection from the carelessness of others."*

Did the Breach Cause Damage?

The claimant must establish that the breach caused the injury complained of. There are complications in establishing causation in the context of comorbidities, diseases, loss of a chance, multiple tortfeasors, combined causes, consecutive cases and intervening acts. The court will start by asking 'but for the defendant's negligence, would the claimant have sustained their injuries?' This is a question of fact and in many cases the answer will be simple and conclusive. Where another cause also contributed to the claimant's injuries, the court may need to decide which was the real or effective cause. This is a question of law. The issue for the court is often whether the chain of causation was broken by an intervening act or event.

Both liability regimes apply in parallel. While it is generally easier for a claimant to establish a claim under the strict liability regime of the Directive, negligence continues to play a role in cases where a claimant seeks to recover damages beyond the limitations and liability caps that apply under the Directive.

Negligence by pharmaceutical companies and device manufacturers has led to some high-profile legal claims in recent years. Too often consumers are injured by a drug or device before it is recalled. It usually takes several lawsuits and consumer complaints to bring attention to a product's dangers. Often the cost of litigation is factored into the retail cost of products in anticipation of litigation. Often a patient's injury or death may be traced to the negligence of a surgeon, or to unforeseen complications, or to an underlying disease. Often it can be traced to the unexpected by-product of faulty design, defective manufacturing and assembly, or inadequate operating instructions of a medical device. Only by reporting the adverse incident, providing Yellow Card feed-back to the MHRA and litigating, can a claimant seek redress. Sadly, it is often too little too late to make any real difference to their health.

Issues

There are a number of issues to consider for implant cases including:

- Manufacturers of business supplies products to consumers need to make sure the products are safe.
- The CPA imposes strict liability on manufacturers of defective products for harm caused by those products. This means that people who are injured by defective products can sue for compensation without having to prove that the manufacturer was negligent.
- There may be more than one party liable under the CPA in respect of the same damage.
- Defendants will seek a confidentiality agreement with any Claimant whose claim is admitted and settled.
- Although liability under the CPA is strict, a manufacturer has a number of defences available if a claim is made.

- A claim cannot be made more than ten years after the product was put into circulation.
- A claimant may succeed in a negligence claim against a manufacturer if she can show a duty of care exists, the duty of care has been breached, the breach created a loss and but for the breach the injury would not have occurred.

CHAPTER SIX
COSMETIC SURGERY NEGLIGENCE

A claimant must commence legal proceedings within 3 years of the treatment otherwise their case is statute barred by virtue of the Limitation Act 1980. The 3-year timescale can run from the date of the incident (surgery or treatment) or from the date of knowledge, which may be some time later. 'Date of knowledge' is the date at which a patient becomes aware that their injury may be attributable in whole or in part to the alleged negligence. This applies only to competent adult claimants. Time limits do not apply to patients who are deemed to lack competence to conduct their own affairs. Formal proceedings may begin on their behalf at any time, regardless of the date of alleged negligence.

Cosmetic surgery negligence claims arise when someone has suffered harm or loss as a consequence of substandard medical treatment. Substandard treatment is defined as *'that which is below the standard you (the patient) could expect from a reasonably competent practitioner'*.

When the claimant had private treatment, the claim is against the individual Surgeon or clinic, if they are vicariously liable. To succeed the Claimant prove on the balance of probabilities that:

- The doctor owed a duty of cares.
- There was a breach of that duty.
- Harm followed as a result (i.e. that causation is established).

The treatment of the patient is assessed using the 'Bolam/Bolitho' and 'Montgomery' standards. This means that the experts will consider the issue of consent against the Montgomery standard and the clinical management of the patient (using Bolam) against that of a responsible body of doctors practicing in the same field. The management of the patient does not have to be the standard of the majority. It just has to be consistent with a responsible body of professional peers and bear logical scrutiny (Bolitho).

The onus is on the claimant to prove that the management of care fell below the standard expected and this caused the harm complained of. The experts should give reasonable and logical evidence for their conclusion. The medical notes should be disclosed early in proceedings in order to assess what exactly occurred and what the claimant was told prior to consenting to the treatment.

Bolam Standard

Bolam v Friern Hospital Management Committee (1957) 1 WLR 582 is the most well-known case in relation to professional standards. For those new to the area of medical negligence it is worth setting out the principles. Many are of the view that it is no longer the leading case being overtaken by Montgomery but it is still an important case and widely used by defendants. Whilst it is no longer applicable for informed consent issues, surgical procedures and management of a patient may still be tested against its standard.

It concerned a patient who sustained fractures during ECT treatment and who alleged that his care whilst under anaesthesia had been negligent. He had not been given a muscle relaxant for the procedure and had not been restrained or warned of the risks of fracture. He lost his case as negligence could not be established. Evidence was provided that at the time of his procedure it was not universal practice to administer muscle relaxation. Contrasting opinions existed as to the benefits of muscle relaxation balanced against the increased risks of the relaxant itself. It was argued that 'if a doctor acted in accordance with a practice that was considered acceptable by a responsible body of doctors that was sufficient' and the claimant must 'show that no reasonable doctor acting in the same circumstances would have acted in that way'.

The 'Bolam standard' is subject to criticism. It has been argued that finding a body of opinion that supports a doctor's actions favours the medical profession. It hands the responsibility for determining negligence back to those same professionals.

Bolitho Standard

In the case of *Bolitho v City and Hackney HA* (1997) 4 ALL ER 771 HL, a child with intermittent croup was not intubated by a paediatric registrar and subsequently suffered hypoxic brain injury from respiratory arrest. The Court found that it is possible to decide that negligence has been proved even if a body of medical opinion suggests otherwise. In Bolitho, it was accepted that failure by the paediatric registrar to attend to the child during an earlier episode of croup was negligent. However, it was argued that even if the registrar had attended, it would not have been appropriate to intubate the child at that point, and that therefore the final subsequent respiratory arrest and hypoxic brain injury sustained by the child could not have been prevented by earlier action. The judge reasoned that the argument that a failure to attend the child would not have made any difference to the eventual outcome was inconclusive and asserted that 'on some occasions, differing bodies of medical opinion could be legitimately distinguished by the court'.

'It is not enough for a defendant to call a number of doctors to say that what he had done or not done was in accord with accepted clinical practice. It is necessary for the judge to consider that evidence and [to] decide whether that clinical practice puts that patient unnecessarily at risk'. Bolitho is not universally applied and Bolam is still considered but both play important roles in establishing negligence. It is useful to bring to the courts attention the extensive practice guidelines produced by bodies like NICE as to how procedures should be undertaken as it allows judges to have objective benchmarks of practice for comparison. It is less easy for doctors to rely on providing a supporting body of opinion that departs from recommendations and guidelines from external agencies.

Consent

A doctor cannot touch a patient without first gaining consent. Trespass to the person can be both a tort (battery) and a crime (assault). If a patient consented to a different procedure to that which took place it could amount to a battery. The advantage of an action in battery is that it is not necessary to establish that any physical harm has been caused by the inadequate disclosure of information.

In the Australian article '*When informed consent goes poorly: a descriptive study of medical negligence claims and patient complaints*' by Gogos et al, they looked at the frequency, characteristics and outcomes of medical legal disputes over information consent. Cosmetic surgeons experienced dispute rates that 'were more than twice those of any other specialty or subspecialty group'. Complaints from cosmetic procedures usually involve allegations that the 'doctor failed to mention or properly explain risks of complications'. Five treatment types account for 46% of all cases: 'procedures on reproductive organs, facial features (excluding eyes), prescription medications, eye surgery and breast surgery'.

The GMC guidance is the starting point when considering consent issues. Their *Guidance for Doctors who offer Cosmetic Interventions* is clear about the duty that doctors have when discussing interventions with patients as is Consent: Patients and Doctors Making Decisions Together. Read and familiarise yourself with both guides. These place professional obligations on doctors regulating conduct.

> ***Guidance for Doctors who offer Cosmetic Interventions***
>
> *Seeking patients' consent*
>
> *15. You must be familiar with the guidance in Consent: patients and doctors making decisions together. In the following paragraphs, we've highlighted key points from the guidance, which are important to protecting patients' interests in relation to cosmetic interventions.*
>
> *Responsibility for seeking consent for cosmetic interventions*
>
> *16. If you are the doctor who will be carrying out the intervention, it is your responsibility to discuss it with the patient and seek their consent – you must not delegate this responsibility. It is essential to a shared understanding of expectations and limitations that consent to a cosmetic intervention is sought by the doctor who will perform it, or supervise its performance by another practitioner.*

Responding to requests for cosmetic interventions

17. If a patient requests an intervention, you must follow the guidance in Consent, including consideration of the patient's medical history. You must ask the patient why they would like to have the intervention and the outcome they hope for, before assessing whether the intervention is appropriate and likely to meet their needs.

18. If you believe the intervention is unlikely to deliver the desired outcome or to be of overall benefit to the patient, you must discuss this with the patient and explain your reasoning. If, after discussion, you still believe the intervention will not be of benefit to the patient, you must not provide it. You should discuss other options available to the patient and respect their right to seek a second opinion.

19. When you discuss interventions and options with a patient, you must consider their vulnerabilities and psychological needs. You must satisfy yourself that the patient's request for the cosmetic intervention is voluntary

20. You must explain any monitoring or follow-up care requirements at the outset. You must tell patients if implanted medical devices may need to be removed or replaced and after how long.

21 You must tell prospective patients if alternative interventions are available that could meet their needs with less risk, including from other practitioners.

Discussing side effects, complications and other risks

22. You must give patients clear, accurate information about the risks of the proposed intervention and any associated procedures, including anaesthesia and sedation, following the guidance in Consent (paragraphs 28–36).*

23. You must talk to the patient about any adverse outcomes that may result from the proposed intervention, paying particular attention to those the patient is most concerned about.† You must talk about the potential adverse physical and psychological impact of the

> *intervention going wrong or failing to meet the patient's expectations. Giving patients time for reflection*

The above guidance should be read and acted upon in accordance with the GMC Guidance *Consent: Patients and Doctors Making Decisions Together* from June 2008. This guidance set the standard by which all doctors should adhere when discussing risks, benefits, alternative treatments or maintaining the status quo when considering treatments. It expands on the guidance in Good medical practice, which requires doctors to be satisfied that they have consent from a patient, or other valid authority, before undertaking any examination or investigation, providing treatment, or involving patients in teaching and research.

It is prudent to refer your medical expert to the specific requirements within the GMC guidance and ask for evidence from within the patients notes that the duties had been complied with. Highlighting the professional responsibility and referring the expert to it is the best way to find evidence of poor consent.

> ***Guidance from GMC Guidance Consent: Patients and Doctors Making Decisions Together***
>
> *Sharing information and discussing treatment options*
>
> *7. The exchange of information between doctor and patient is central to good decision-making. How much information you share with patients will vary, depending on their individual circumstances. You should tailor your approach to discussions with patients according to:*
>
> > *a. their needs, wishes and priorities*
> >
> > *b. their level of knowledge about, and understanding of, their condition, prognosis and the treatment options*
> >
> > *c. the nature of their condition*
> >
> > *d. the complexity of the treatment, and*

e. the nature and level of risk associated with the investigation or treatment.

8. *You should not make assumptions about:*

a. the information a patient might want or need

b. the clinical or other factors a patient might consider significant, or

c. a patient's level of knowledge or understanding of what is proposed.

9. *You must give patients the information they want or need about:*

a. the diagnosis and prognosis

b. any uncertainties about the diagnosis or prognosis, including options for further investigations

c. options for treating or managing the condition, including the option not to treat

d. the purpose of any proposed investigation or treatment and what it will involve

e. the potential benefits, risks and burdens, and the likelihood of success, for each option; this should include information, if available, about whether the benefits or risks are affected by which organisation or doctor is chosen to provide care

f. whether a proposed investigation or treatment is part of a research programme or is an innovative treatment designed specifically for their benefit

g. the people who will be mainly responsible for and involved in their care, what their roles are, and to what extent students may be involved

h. their right to refuse to take part in teaching or research i. their right to seek a second opinion

j. any bills they will have to pay

k. any conflicts of interest that you, or your organisation, may have

l. any treatments that you believe have greater potential benefit for the patient than those you or your organisation can offer.

10. You should explore these matters with patients, listen to their concerns, ask for and respect their views, and encourage them to ask questions

11. You should check whether patients have understood the information they have been given, and whether or not they would like more information before making a decision. You must make it clear that they can change their mind about a decision at any time.

Answering questions

12. You must answer patients' questions honestly and, as far as practical, answer as fully as they wish.

Reasons for not sharing information with patients

13. No one else can make a decision on behalf of an adult who has capacity. If a patient asks you to make decisions on their behalf or wants to leave decisions to a relative, partner, friend, carer or another person close to them, you should explain that it is still important that they understand the options open to them, and what the treatment will involve. If they do not want this information, you should try to find out why.

14. If, after discussion, a patient still does not want to know in detail about their condition or the treatment, you should respect their wishes, as far as possible. But you must still give them the information they need in order to give their consent to a proposed investigation or treatment. This is likely to include what the investigation or treatment aims to achieve and what it will involve, for example: whether the procedure is invasive; what level of pain or discomfort they might experience, and what can be done to minimise it; anything they should do to prepare for the investigation or treatment; and if it involves any serious risks.

15. If a patient insists that they do not want even this basic information, you must explain the potential consequences of them not having it, particularly if it might mean that their consent is not valid. You must record the fact that the patient has declined this information. You must also make it clear that they can change their mind and have more information at any time.

16. You should not withhold information necessary for making decisions for any other reason, including when a relative, partner, friend or carer asks you to, unless you believe that giving it would cause the patient serious harm. In this context 'serious harm' means more than that the patient might become upset or decide to refuse treatment.

17. If you withhold information from the patient you must record your reason for doing so in the patient's medical records, and you must be prepared to explain and justify your decision. You should regularly review your decision, and consider whether you could give information to the patient later, without causing them serious harm.

Sharing information

18. How you discuss a patient's diagnosis, prognosis and treatment options is often as important as the information itself. You should:

a. share information in a way that the patient can understand and, whenever possible, in a place and at a time when they are best able to understand and retain it

b. give information that the patient may find distressing in a considerate way

c. involve other members of the healthcare team in discussions with the patient, if appropriate6 d give the patient time to reflect, before and after they make a decision, especially if the information is complex or what you are proposing involves significant risks

e. make sure the patient knows if there is a time limit on making their decision, and who they can contact in the healthcare team if they have any questions or concerns.

19. You should give information to patients in a balanced way. If you recommend a particular treatment or course of action, you should explain your reasons for doing so. But you must not put pressure on a patient to accept your advice.

20. You may need to support your discussions with patients by using written material, or visual or other aids. If you do, you must make sure the material is accurate and up to date.

21. You should check whether the patient needs any additional support to understand information, to communicate their wishes, or to make a decision. You should bear in mind that some barriers to understanding and communication may not be obvious; for example, a patient may have unspoken anxieties, or may be affected by pain or other underlying problems. You must make sure, wherever practical, that arrangements are made to give the patient any necessary support. This might include, for example: using an advocate or interpreter; asking those close to the patient about the patient's communication needs; or giving the patient a written or audio record of the discussion and any decisions that were made

Responsibility for seeking a patient's consent

26. If you are the doctor undertaking an investigation or providing treatment, it is your responsibility to discuss it with the patient. If this is not practical, you can delegate the responsibility to someone else, provided you make sure that the person you delegate to: a is suitably trained and qualified b has sufficient knowledge of the proposed investigation or treatment, and understands the risks involved c understands, and agrees to act in accordance with, the guidance in this booklet.

27. If you delegate, you are still responsible for making sure that the patient has been given enough time and information to make an informed decision, and has given their consent, before you start any investigation or treatment.

Discussing side effects, complications and other risks

28. Clear, accurate information about the risks of any proposed investigation or treatment, presented in a way patients can understand, can help them make informed decisions. The amount of information about risk that you should share with patients will depend on the individual patient and what they want or need to know. Your discussions with patients should focus on their individual situation and the risk to them.

29. In order to have effective discussions with patients about risk, you must identify the adverse outcomes that may result from the proposed options. This includes the potential outcome of taking no action. Risks can take a number of forms, but will usually be:

a. side effects

b. complications

c. failure of an intervention to achieve the desired aim.

Risks can vary from common but minor side effects, to rare but serious adverse outcomes possibly resulting in permanent disability or death.

30. In assessing the risk to an individual patient, you must consider the nature of the patient's condition, their general health and other circumstances. These are variable factors that may affect the likelihood of adverse outcomes occurring.

31. You should do your best to understand the patient's views and preferences about any proposed investigation or treatment, and the adverse outcomes they are most concerned about. You must not make assumptions about a patient's understanding of risk or the importance they attach to different outcomes. You should discuss these issues with your patient.

32. You must tell patients if an investigation or treatment might result in a serious adverse outcome, even if the likelihood is very small. You should also tell patients about less serious side effects or complications if they occur frequently, and explain what the patient should do if they experience any of them.

33. You must give information about risk in a balanced way. You should avoid bias, and you should explain the expected benefits as well as the potential burdens and risks of any proposed investigation or treatment.

34. You must use clear, simple and consistent language when discussing risks with patients. You should be aware that patients may understand information about risk differently from you. You should check that the patient understands the terms that you use, particularly when describing the seriousness, frequency and likelihood of an adverse outcome. You should use simple and accurate written information or visual or other aids to explain risk, if they will help the patient to understand.

35. If a patient does not want to know about the possible risks of a proposed investigation or treatment, you must follow the guidance in paragraphs 13–17.

36. You must keep up to date with developments in your area of practice, which may affect your knowledge and understanding of the risks associated with the investigations or treatments that you provide.

Recording decisions

51. You must use the patient's medical records or a consent form to record the key elements of your discussion with the patient. This should include the information you discussed, any specific requests by the patient, any written, visual or audio information given to the patient, and details of any decisions that were made.

Mental Capacity

Deciding whether someone is legally competent to make decisions regarding their own treatment requires an assessment of their mental capacity. The assessed capacity required for legal competence increases with the seriousness of what is at stake. Patient autonomy is being balanced against best interests. When a patient chooses a course of action, it is not just mental capacity that doctors should consider against that patient's best interests. Any attempt rigidly to define a group of legally incompetent people is likely to have adverse consequences for patients and the care they receive. Central to any discussion of mental capacity is whether the patient has competence to understand and consent to what is to take place and the risks and complications involved.

The Mental Capacity Act 2005 provides a legal framework for making decisions in relation to people who lack capacity. It clarifies:

- who can make decisions, including decisions about medical care and treatment, for people who are unable to decide for themselves;

- how those decisions should be made.

Section 1 of the Act sets out five statutory principles that apply to any action taken and decisions made under the Act. These are:

1. a person must be assumed to have capacity unless it is established that they lack capacity

2. a person is not to be treated as unable to make a decision unless all practicable steps to help him do so have been taken without success

3. a person is not to be treated as unable to make a decision merely because he makes an unwise decision

4. an act done, or decision made, under the Act for or on behalf of a person who lacks capacity must be done, or made, in his best interests

5. before the act is done, or the decision is made, regard must be had to whether the purpose for which it is needed can be as effectively achieved in a way that is less restrictive of the person's rights and freedom of action.

In this Act, people lack capacity in relation to a particular matter if, at the material time, they are unable to make a decision for themselves in relation to the matter because of an impairment of, or a disturbance in the functioning of, the mind or brain (section 2(1)). Doctors and other healthcare professionals must have regard to the supporting Code of Practice, which explains how the Act should work on a day to day basis and sets out the steps that those using and interpreting it should follow when assessing a person's capacity, or in reaching a decision in the best interests of a person who does not have capacity.

It is worthy of note that the normal rule of the common law (*Imperial Loan Co v Stone* (1892) 1 QB 599) was that a contract entered into by a person who lacked capacity or was a minor was not void, but was voidable. If your client lacks capacity then it is worth considering at what point that capacity was lost and the implications for the contract and consent to treatment.

There are several important decisions relating to the issue of treatment for persons who lack capacity. In Aintree University Hospitals NHS Foundation Trust (Respondent) v James (Appellant) [2013] UKSC 67 the court held that the test, per S.1(4) of the Act is whether it is in the patient's "best interests" to provide the treatment, having regard to (a) the checklist set out at S4, and the 2007 Code of Practice. The "best interests" test is subjective in that considering the 'wishes and feelings of the patient the court must consider that patient's wishes and feelings not what a reasonable patient would think'. It is the patient's point of view which is important. The important question is 'whether it is lawful to give the treatment, not whether it is lawful to withhold it'. It is only lawful to provide invasive treatment with the patient's consent. It is not unlawful for a Doctor not to give treatment where the patient (of full capacity) refuses it. With an incapacitated patient (i.e. one who is not able to give consent) it is only lawful to give invasive treatment where 'it is necessary in that patient's best interests'.

Here arises the implication for cosmetic surgery. One must look at the welfare of the patient in the widest sense, not just medical, but social and psychological; consider the nature, invasiveness, degree of pain, and possible outcomes of the treatment. What would the patients attitude to treatment be? These issues will usually arise following treatment to a person who lacked capacity and the extent to which the psychological profiling identified the lack of capacity.

Montgomery Standard

As a result of this ground-breaking case we have the adage 'doctors advise – patients decide'. Reasonable treatments require risks and benefits to be discussed and advised upon. Reasonable risks and material risks are 'significant' when a reasonable prudent patient would attach significance. The duty of care now is to protect autonomy. Alternatives to surgery include doing nothing and advise that this is an option. The 2015 Supreme Court decision in *Montgomery v NHS Lanarkshire* [2015] UKSC 11, has significant implications for doctor-patient communications, information disclosure and informed consent. Yet when you consider the obligations and positive requirements set out by the GMC, the stance the court took was only that which doctors 'should' have been doing since 2008.

In this case, Nadine Montgomery, was awarded £5.25m compensation for the brain damage to her baby during birth. There had been a 16-year legal fight culminating in the Supreme Court decision. Mrs Montgomery had type 1 diabetes which increased the risk of her having a larger than average baby, a risk which was compounded by her own small stature. The increased risk of complications from a vaginal birth included shoulder dystocia. In this case the baby's shoulder got stuck and during the procedures to deliver her baby suffered oxygen deprivation. This resulted in brain damage and cerebral palsy. Mrs Montgomery had expressed concerns about her ability to deliver her baby safely given her diabetes and indicated that had she been advised of the risks, she would have chosen to have a caesarean section. Her obstetrician made the decision not to discuss the risks of shoulder dystocia or to discuss a caesarean. The obstetrician's view was that if the condition had been mentioned, most women would elect for a Caesarean section and this would not be in their interest.

The claim failed in the first instance. The court found that the obstetrician had not been negligent either in her advice or her management of the labour. When the case reached the Supreme Court, the principal issue was whether the obstetrician's failure to warn Mrs Montgomery of the risk of shoulder dystocia was negligent.

Prior to Montgomery the 'Bolam test' of negligence was applied not just to *diagnosis and treatment* but also to *advice*. The question in Montgomery was whether it provided the correct test applied to the doctor's duty to *advise*. In *Sidaway v Board of Governors of the Bethlem Royal Hospital and the Maudsley Hospital* [1985] AC 871 the House of Lords held that it did although the minority view of Lord Scarman was that it did not. The Supreme Court in Montgomery noted that English courts had nevertheless recently been moving in a different direction and, when it came to advice, the Bolam test had been undermined by some recent decisions. There had been a change in the social, medical and legal landscape since Sidaway. People were now regarded as autonomous bearers of rights, governing their own lives and making choices for themselves. They had more access to medical information through the internet and information leaflets. Doctors also received professional guidance which gave greater emphasis to the concerns and choices of patients (since 2008). Further there had been developments in Human Rights law and the courts were increasingly conscious of the value of self-determination particularly in cases involving issues of withdrawal of treatment.

The Supreme Court therefore rejected the application of the Bolam test in relation to the doctor's duty to advise. The test was not whether a doctor acted in accordance with a practice accepted as proper by a responsible body of medical practitioners but was based instead on what a 'particular patient would expect to know'.

'An adult person of sound mind is entitled to decide which, if any, of the available forms of treatment to undergo, and her consent must be obtained before treatment interfering with her bodily integrity is undertaken. The doctor is therefore under a duty to take reasonable care to ensure that the patient is aware of any material risks involved in any recommended treatment, and of any reasonable alternative or variant treatments. The test of materiality is whether, in the circumstances of the particular case, a reasonable person in the patient's position would be likely to attach significance to the risk, or the doctor is or should reasonably be aware that the particular patient would be likely to attach significance to it.'

Whether a risk should be regarded as material depends on the patient's perspective rather than the doctor's. It is fact-sensitive, depending on the particular patient's characteristics. There were highlighted 3 exceptions to the general rule:

1. Where a patient tells a doctor that she does not want to know the risks (but see the GMC guidance on this issue above)

2. The 'therapeutic exception': i.e. if disclosure of the risk would be seriously detrimental to a patient's health; and

3. Necessity i.e. an unconscious patient requiring urgent treatment.

Mrs Montgomery was found to have the right to be advised of the risk of shoulder dystocia, and decide what risks she was prepared to take. The court accepted that she would have opted for a Caesarean section with proper advice. It awarded her damages of £5.25 million.

This is a very significant decision. The Supreme Court has rejected a clinician-centred and paternalistic approach to consent replacing paternalism with patient autonomy. Standard consent forms are unlikely to be adequate and the time available to fully discuss the options needs to be increased. Doctors need to ensure they have more detailed discussions with their patients and record those discussions.

It will be interesting to see if patients elect for more expensive treatments which hospitals may wish to avoid, such as an increase in diabetic women seeking Caesarean sections. This may be a cause of concern for the NHS which is constantly striving to save money. In *Thefaut v Johnston* [2017] EWHC 497 (QB) the claimant was successful on the basis that she had not given her informed consent to surgery. The Judge found that she was not warned about material risks of discectomy surgery and that, had she been properly advised, she would not have undergone surgery. The Defendant was found liable for the consequences of the surgery, including the operation which he undertook and subsequent revision surgery undertaken by a different surgeon.

The decision in Montgomery illustrates the Courts finally catching up with the regulatory requirements which had been in place since 2008. The Court as now reinforced the professional obligations as legal obligations. It is prudent therefore to refer your medical expert to the specific requirements within the GMC guidance and Montgomery. Ask for evidence from within the patients notes that the duties had been complied with. Highlighting the detailed responsibility and referring the expert back to the regulatory requirements is the best way to find evidence of poor consent.

Whilst patient autonomy now takes precedence in decision-making, doctors are under no legal or ethical obligation to agree to a patient's request for or rejection of treatment, if they consider the treatment is not in the patient's best interests (see Mr Leslie Burke v GMC [2005] EWCA Civ 1003 and *Re T (Adult)* [1992] 4 All ER 649). In this case a 20-year-old pregnant woman, was injured in a car accident and developed complications that required blood transfusions. She did not indicate on admission that she was opposed to receiving transfusions but after spending some time with her mother, who was a practicing Jehovah's Witness, she decided to refuse the treatment. The Court of Appeal considered that she had been under pressure from her mother and under heavy medication which impaired her ability to decide about the transfusions. The Court allowed the blood transfusions to proceed. A patient's consent to treatment may not be valid if it is given under pressure or duress exerted by another person.

In the cases since Montgomery it is clear, that obstetrics will be the area of medicine most affected by the Montgomery decision. Mothers have a long time to consider their mode of birth and risks associated with it combined with any other risk factors inherent in their or their baby's health. There will always be the conflict between the medical view that a vaginal delivery is appropriate and safe and the wishes of mothers in labour to have a Caesarean section.

Montgomery defines the nature of the duty to advise but in the subsequent case of Tasmin there was a potential conflict between the scope of that duty from the perspective of the medical profession and the patient (*Tasmin* v Barts Health NHS Trust [2015]). It is still difficult for Claimants to establish claims based on consent but they will be greatly assisted where the evidence from treating doctors is either that, had they been asked they would have agreed an alternative course of treatment or that patients in general would elect for that treatment (Montgomery).

In the case of *SXX v Liverpool Women's NHS Foundation Trust* [2015] EWHC 4072 one twin was delivered by forceps and suffered an intracranial haemorrhage which caused a neurological disability, whilst his twin sister was delivered by emergency Caesarean section. The mother had been concerned about the risks of vaginal birth particularly given that the father's brother had lost one of two twins at birth 7 years previously. As a result she raised her concerns when booking a scan and the consultant obstetrician subsequently wrote in the notes, 'For elective Caesarean section if wishes'. However, when she went into labour the midwife persuaded her to have a vaginal delivery and did not refer to a consultant. It was alleged that there was a breach of duty in failing to take due account of the mother's wishes.

Experts in obstetrics and midwifery agreed that the mother should have been referred for a Caesarean had she requested one. She was also able to adduce helpful evidence from the consultant at trial who said he would have agreed to a Caesarean in the circumstances, despite a vaginal birth probably being safe. The court found that there was a breach of duty in failing to refer discussion of the mode of delivery to the consultant who would have agreed to a Caesarean thereby avoiding the injury to the child.

In *Tasmin v Barts Health NHS Trust* [2015] the claimant was born by emergency Caesarean section. Minutes before birth the umbilical cord tightened around her neck resulting in a profound hypoxic/ischaemic episode and she suffered a severe brain injury which left her seriously disabled. She alleged negligence in the management of her delivery and a failure to obtain adequate consent from her mother to persevering with labour rather than undergoing a Caesarean section when it became clear that Mother was struggling. The key issues arose during the period between 21.40 and 22.30 when the registrar had failed to interpret CTG readings. The registrar proceeded with Syntocinon infusions when the correct course of action would have been to take samples of the foetal blood. The claimant alleged that at this stage there should have been a discussion with her Mother about the risks of the pathological trace and the alternative course of management by Caesarean section. In the absence of such a discussion the decision to proceed with vaginal delivery was made without her consent and was negligent. Mr Justice Jay preferred the Defendant's expert evidence that good medical practice required foetal blood sampling before any consideration of Caesarean section, the pathological CTG not by itself being diagnostic of hypoxia which might lead to acidosis. However, the claimant's case was one of consent and thus cannot be resolved solely on the basis of expert evidence. Her mother should have been advised of the material risk of injury and been able to elect for a Caesarean at this stage.

The court found that because CTG is not a diagnostic tool, there could not be a sensible discussion of the options before foetal blood sampling had been done. More significantly the risk of serious injury was negligible, of the order of 1:1,000. He held that this was not a material risk, citing A v East Kent Hospitals NHS Foundation Trust [2015] EWHC where Dingemans J described a risk of 1:1,000 as 'theoretical, negligible or background'. However he preferred to formulate the risk as being 'too low to be material'. The claim therefore failed.

How do we measure risk and do we measure it at all? The Supreme Court in Montgomery explicitly said that what amounted to a material risk was **not** a matter of percentages. Thus, what is important to one patient may not be to another. Mr Justice Jay found that a risk of 1:1,000 was too low to be material but in Montgomery the risk of shoulder dystocia had been 9-10% and that in itself presented a risk of significant injury. However the risk of a prolonged hypoxia had been 0.1% or 1:1,000, the same as in Tasmin.

The problem with looking at risk in percentage terms is that it looks only at one of two components: the probability as opposed to the severity of injury. It is what is significant to the patient which is important. 0.1% may be a negligible risk in the context of a minor injury but many mothers would regard it as significant if it could give rise to their baby having a lifelong disability. Percentages do not take into account factors which are specific to the particular patient. Sadly, no such factors were identified in Tasmin.

If the case turned on when to hold a discussion of options for management of labour then there is a need to set out clearly from the beginning the management of labour and what choices can be made depending on the events that occur. Providing mothers with information before labour commences assists the consent process, so that in the event of distress or complication everyone is aware of the choices made. At present it appears that the Bolam standard applies to events during labour, rather than Montgomery however, this position may change.

There have been cases where the claimant has simply failed to establish an absence of consent on the facts. In *Julie Connolly v Croydon Health Services NHS Trust* [2015] EWHC 1339 the claimant failed to establish that she had not been properly warned of the risks of an angiogram or withdrawn her consent to continue treatment when a complication arose. Whilst in *MC, JC v Birmingham Women's NHS Foundation Trust [2016]* EWCH 1334 the claimants failed to establish on the facts that the mother had not given consent to induction of labour.

Most recently the Court of Appeal confirmed that the *Bolam* standard has no place when determining whether there has been a breach of duty in the consenting process. In *Webster v. Burton Hospitals NHS Foundation Trust* [2017] EWCA Civ 62 during the course of his birth in 2003, Sebastian sustained a hypoxic ischaemic brain injury as a result of a relatively short period of umbilical cord compression leaving him with cerebral palsy, involving profound physical and cognitive impairments. Breach of duty was admitted by the Defendant Trust. It was also admitted that the Consultant Obstetrician in charge of the pregnancy should have arranged a further ultrasound scan every two weeks as the baby was small for the gestational age. The main issue to be determined was causation, i.e. what would have been shown had further ultrasound scanning taken place and what should have happened as a consequence?

The Consultant's evidence was that the results of any further scans would not have altered his management plan, although he accepted that the results would have been discussed with mum. The Defendant argued that the course of events that took place would always have taken place and that the unfortunate outcome would always have occurred. At first instance applying *Bolam* for breach of duty, the High Court found that there 'was a reasonable and responsible body of Obstetric opinion who would have acted in the same way as the Consultant would have done, i.e. they would also not have altered their management plan' and the case was dismissed. The Court of Appeal considered *Montgomery* and stated that the *Bolam* test no longer applies to issues of consent in clinical negligence claims. The 'new' test for breach of duty in consent claims as per *Montgomery* is whether the doctor has explained the material risks that:

1. An objective reasonable person would attach significance to; and

2. *The particular patient* would attach significance to.

In applying the *Bolam* test, the Court of Appeal therefore held that the Judge at first instance had erred. Applying the *Montgomery* standard, the Court of Appeal found that the Consultant would or should have informed mum that the likely combination of features on any further scans was associated with increased risks of delaying the labour. The Court found that mum would have attached significant to those risks on the basis that:

- her evidence was clear that if there had been 'any suggestion of risk I would have wanted him to be delivered';

- she had a university degree in nursing; and

- she was willing to take responsibility for her pregnancy as demonstrated by her decision to leave hospital earlier in the pregnancy against the advice of the doctors.

The Court found that had the material risks been explained she would likely have opted for an earlier delivery on 27 December 2002, which would in turn have avoided all Sebastian's injuries.

It is now clearer than ever that the court is supporting the Montgomery standard and the *Bolam* test now has no place in the determination of breach of duty when considering issues of consent. When considering the subjective limb of the test, i.e. whether the Claimant themselves would attach significance to a risk that is considered 'material', the Courts have indicated that they will take a very wide range of factors into consideration, including the Claimant's education, conduct throughout the relevant treatment and evidence during the litigation. Doctors are, and have been since at least 2008, under a duty to understand the particular, and personal, concerns of their patients.

The court's decision in Montgomery makes it clear that in cosmetic surgery claims, any intervention or treatment must be based on a shared decision-making process, ensuring that the patient is aware of all options and supported to make an informed choice. Standardized information about procedures and their risks and benefits is the way to deliver shared decision making. An extension of the NICE guidelines is needed for cosmetic surgery procedures. Doctors and patients need access to the same information. Most importantly sufficient time is needed to explain the risks and benefits of a recommended course of action (and the other options available). An opportunity to reflect on the options before deciding what is best for them is vital. The law on consent is moving faster than clinical practice and many practitioners are failing to document valid consent. Despite the professional obligations and the case law that now exists, the paperwork and time given to patients to discuss consent is lacking.

When reviewing the claimant's medical records check the: management plan, explanations given and patient responses. Where there is evidence of all three processes in the records it is usually evidence that there has been good communication of consent. The less that there is written, then the less likely it is that the time was spent discussing risks, benefits and complications. Before litigating seek a duty of candour request to determine the usual practice if the notes are lacking. This way the evidence of what did happen and what should always happen can be reflected upon against the law and GMC guidance.

The records should highlight: what is being sought, what the patient thinks, the steps to be taken, what to expect and the follow up. The GMC states that the records should include 'the decisions made and actions agreed, the information given and any drugs prescribed or other investigation or treatment'. At present, there is no clinical reasoning or diagnosis required when prescribing medication but that does depend on the purpose of the medication.

Information can be provided in leaflets, consent forms or briefly noted. Consent forms are useful as they convey an accurate record of the explanation. Have all available options been discussed? The challenge for the doctor is for the information to be sufficient and proportionate and for the patient to understand the risks of what may occur and what to do about it if it does occur. If there were several consultations, what is described in these consultations and what was the purpose of them?

Failure to follow the law could potentially be used more widely to overturn the presumption that a doctor's word will be preferred over the patients. After all the doctor is seeing several patients each day and cannot recall the details of each patient and what was discussed (unless it is written down) whereas the patient is only concerned about their own welfare and is seeking out the treatment. Their recollection of the encounter with the doctor will be pronounced.

If the doctor refuses a duty of candour request, made inadequate records, failed to discuss options and did not record patient responses, they are going to find it difficult to persuade a court that the initial consultation satisfied the rules on consent. In the case of *Karen Turner v Mr Nigel Carver* (2016) the scope of the duty of care owed to cosmetic surgery patients, the role of the consent process and the importance of following instructions were examined. In this case, the claimant sought breast augmentation surgery from the Defendant. She had previously had such procedures and wanted to increase her breast size. For several weeks, they communicated over the surgical options, the size of the implants and the risks of surgery. The Claimant was provided with information sheets setting out information. Following surgery, she returned to the Defendant for liposuction some three months later. At seven-months post breast surgery, she needed a procedure to change the positon of one of the breast implants. She experienced a serious complication with a haematoma requiring emergency surgical drainage. She complained about the outcome achieved from the first operation that she had been happy with, but stated firstly that the breasts were not large enough and then that they were too large. The claimant sought compensation and the matter went to trial. Her case was that she had not been given 'adequate information about the risks of surgery'. If she had, she would not have undergone the operation. She stated that the implants were 'far too large and produced an unnatural result'. The Court examined the notes of the consent-taking and found that they were not as full as they could be. However, looking at the matter as a whole, they believed that the Defendant had both orally and through the provision of detailed information sheets, provided sufficient information about the risks. These were the basis upon which the Claimant had consented. What is important are the detailed discussions and precise instructions passing between the claimant and defendant which assisted the successful defence of the action.

The Claimant further alleged that the breasts were too large and whether it was incumbent on the Defendant to refuse to insert the relatively large implants that the claimant had requested. The court rejected this contention and preferred the evidence of the defence expert who stated that 'negligence would occur when the cosmetic outcome went outside the very wide range of natural human variation' and in this case, it did not. Being unhappy with the outcome of cosmetic surgery was not due to negligence but 'buyers remorse'.

It is worthy of note that this case also considered contributory negligence in a cosmetic surgery action. It stated that where the facts allow it would be prepared to make a finding and she would have lost 66% of the compensation due to her contributory negligence. This was because of the haematoma issue and the surgery that ensued. The court found that she had been advised on several occasions 'not to engage in strenuous exercise for several weeks after surgery' but had been to the gym and this had 'probably' been strenuous exercise which most likely caused her haematoma.

This case is a good example of the courts approach to the consent process and how much reliance is placed on documented discussions of risks, whether information leaflets are helpful and the conduct of both parties leading up to surgery and post-surgery. It is clear that the best defence a cosmetic surgeon can have is well constructed notes. Clear consultation notes, advice letters and leaflets, communications with the patient, consent documents, operative notes, laboratory results all demonstrate a good exchange of information. Bad notes demonstrate hurried staff, overburdened organisation and lip service paid to regulatory guidance. Great notes represent great surgeons (most of the time).

Smoking

Studies have shown that nicotine, a potent vasoconstrictor, can significantly compromise the capillary flow to the skin. When the skin has been lifted from its normal blood supply and then laid back in part or in whole, the resumption of a capillary network is key to its survival. It is critical that post surgery the new blood flow achieves the best outcome across the incision. Nicotine is the enemy of skin survival whether through cigarettes, patches or gum. If a case is pursued for poor outcome of surgery, it is prudent to establish if the claimant has a nicotine habit. Undoubtedly the Defendant will raise the issue of smoking and its contribution to the surgical outcome. As we have seen, the courts are now willing to consider contributory negligence. However, the surgeon needs to have discussed the risks and recorded the discussion for a defence to succeed otherwise the argument will be weak. A claimant may state that had they known that stopping smoking would aid the recovery and prevent complications then they would have stopped.

Car Accident

If the claimant has been involved in a car or other high impact accident since the implantation surgery where the claimant suffered trauma to the chest, then this may harm her case of alleged fault. The defendant may be able to argue that their implants may have been damaged by the impact of the accident. This is likely to be dependent upon the facts of the individual case. For example, some claimants received representations that the product was so durable as to be virtually indestructible. However, if the rupture or its symptoms are identified immediately after the crash then the defendant will almost certainly resist the case.

Multiple Procedures

When multiple procedures are scheduled, it is important to have each one consented to separately. The risks of an uplift are different to the risks relating to implants and the risks of those procedures combined should be discussed. Even where it states 'and other procedures deemed necessary' it is necessary for the Doctor to discuss what those procedures may be, why they may occur, the risks/complications and what the proposed course of action would be. For example, when performing an abdominoplasty a doctor may also use liposuction on the patients abdomen in order to achieve a better final result. The Claimant should know that liposuction will take place and what the risks, benefits and complications of liposuction are in order to provide informed consent.

Scars

Cosmetic surgery creates scars. Few procedures can be done laparoscopically and scarring is very much down to genetics. Whilst surgeon skill plays a part, it is down to skin colour, thickness of the dermis, infections, previous scarring, skin tension and delayed healing. It is prudent to discuss the extent of the scarring. Many Claimants who feel that they have not achieved their desired result and who are left with prominent scarring that they had not bargained for will seek redress. How often are scars discussed? What options are available to claimants to achieve the desired look without surgical intervention? The truth is that there is little money to be made in telling claimants not to undertake the surgery they seek. Always discuss with the claimant their expectation about scarring and what, if anything, was discussed with their surgeon.

In 'Factors influencing judicial decisions in medical disputes in plastic surgery' Vila-Nova da Silva DB et al looked at lawsuits in Brazil following breast surgery, abdominoplasty, rhinoplasty and liposuction. The most common complaints were scarring and contour, general dissatisfaction and complications. In all cases with 'good quality records' the surgeons were found not negligent. There was a significant correlation between decisions favouring the surgeon and written consent documentation. The better the records and consent documentation then more likely that the Claimant lost.

Although these articles looked at data from abroad, the principles apply equally to the UK. The success or otherwise of a Claimant's case is heavily dependent on the quality of the surgeon's records. Surgeons should pay special attention to obtaining informed consent because it is a double-edged sword. It has clinical purpose for doctors and patients but it is also a major litigation strategy for solicitors.

Duty to Advise

The case of *David Spencer v Hillingdon Hospital NHS Trust* [2015] is interesting as it considers a doctor's duty to advise which is particularly of use in cosmetic surgery claims. The claimant underwent surgery to repair an inguinal hernia. After discharge from hospital he developed complications in the form of a deep vein thrombosis and pulmonary embolism on each lung. He claimed he had not been warned of these complications. He had not been alerted to the significance of symptoms, such as pain and swelling in the leg, heat or discolouration, altered sensation, shortness of breath and chest pain and what to do should they develop. He therefore did not recognise the onset of the condition and delayed in seeking medical help. As a result, his condition was worse than it would have been, given proper advice. It was not his case, however, that had he been warned of the risks he would not have undergone the repair.

The court was guided by the decision in Montgomery in defining the extent of the duty to advise. It commented,

> *'there is force in the contention...that the basic principles – and the resulting duty of care – defined in Montgomery are likely to be applied to all aspects of the provision of advice given to patients by medical and nursing staff. Insofar as the judgment in Montgomery emphasizes the need for a court to take into account a patient's view as well as the doctor's the significance of information for a patient I consider it relevant to the facts of this case.'*

The case is therefore one which demonstrates the impact of Montgomery in defining what advice should be given even in cases where consent was not involved. It is not clear however that the decision in Spencer would have been any different had the Bolam test been applied to that duty. So often in cosmetic cases, patients are unaware of certain aspects of the procedure they are undertaking and the need to say, have implants removed and replaced, to not go to the gym and undertake strenuous exercise, to not smoke even.

Absence of Consent

In *Border v Lewisham and Greenwich NHS Trust* [2015] the Court of Appeal (before the Montgomery decision) highlighted the importance of considering not only whether a treatment is acceptable but whether the patient has consented at all. The claimant was a 64 year old woman who had fractured her right humerus. She was taken to A&E at Queen Elizabeth Hospital where the duty SHO wanted to put an IV line into her arm which was standard procedure. Although there was no immediate need to do so it ensured that staff would be ready should an emergency arise. He was unable to use her injured right arm and normal practice would have been to use the left. However, she told the doctor she had recently undergone a left mammectomy and axillary node clearance in the left arm thus there was a risk of oedema if the left arm was used. The options were either to go ahead using the left arm or to wait and see whether a cannula would be needed later. There was a conflict of evidence as to exactly what happened. The judge accepted the claimant's account that the doctor in effect made a 'quick and silent calculation' and only communicated with the claimant to the extent of saying something like, 'I'm sorry, but we really need to put it in the right arm'. She hardly realised what was happening until it was done. She went on to develop a permanent and serious case of oedema in the left arm which caused significant disability.

At first instance the judge found that the decision to insert a line in the left arm rather than adopting a 'wait and see' approach accorded with accepted practice. An experienced consultant might feel able to take a calculated risk to wait and see but it would be a 'bold decision for a senior house officer'. His action did not in itself amount to a breach of duty. The claim therefore failed and on Appeal the claimant raised a case which had not been argued at trial. She argued (and this was contested by the Defendant) that there had been a finding of fact that the doctor had not obtained her consent before inserting the cannula. On that ground, there was a breach of duty and she was entitled to judgment. The fact that the doctor acted in accordance with accepted practice did not mean he was entitled to do so without consent.

The Court of Appeal noted that allegations based on consent were within the scope of her pleaded case even if they had not been raised at trial. She was therefore entitled to contend on appeal that lack of consent entailed a breach of duty:

> *'A finding of absence of consent to the insertion of the cannula leads inexorably to a finding of breach of duty in inserting it'.*

The Court of Appeal agreed. It granted a declaration that the doctor was in breach of his duty in inserting the cannula without the claimant's consent. It refused her permission to amend the pleadings to add a claim of trespass to the person, a finding which would have short-circuited the issue of causation.

This case highlights the importance of properly pleading all issues but also establishes consent issues. Had she pleaded trespass to the person the claim would have succeeded without having to establish that with proper advice she would not have consented. The case also highlights the importance of raising consent as an issue in appropriate cases. This was a case where the medical decision was not negligent but proceeding without consent was.

CHAPTER SEVEN
MATERIAL CONTRIBUTION

The case of *Dr Sido John v Central Manchester and Manchester Children's University Hospitals NHS Foundation Trust* [2016] EWHC 407 is an extremely important case. It's the first judgment following *Williams v The Bermuda Hospitals Board* [2016] UKPC 4 to address the doctrine of material contribution.

The Claimant was a General Practitioner and prison doctor who developed an intra-cranial infection at the age of 16 that required a left-sided craniotomy. He was left with mid, right-sided hemiparesis which required him to use his left hand (he had been right-handed) and caused him certain mobility difficulties. On the 23rd December 2007 he was climbing the stairs and lost his footing. He fell backwards and lay there for some 2 hours covered in vomit and 'in a bad way'. An ambulance was called and the he was taken to Manchester Royal Infirmary (MRI) where he was admitted at about 6.52am in the morning. He was triaged and a management plan was formulated which included CT scanning of the Claimant's brain. The Claimant's CT scan was then cancelled despite the Claimant developing warning signs that he was suffering a head injury including confusion and disorientation. He was then transferred from A&E to another ward and the seriousness of the Claimant's situation was recognised and the CT scan reordered. This was at 1.12pm, some 6 1/2 hours after he was admitted to hospital.

The CT scan showed that he had an acute sub-dural haematoma, causing raised intra-cranial pressure, necessitating his immediate re-admission to 'resus' and transfer to a specialist neurosurgery team at another hospital. The Claimant's condition was radically deteriorating, its seriousness emphasized by the MRI nurse taking care of him who stated that 'It's a total priority we need to get this man to theatre, it's a matter of life or death really.' At 3.17pm an ambulance was requested to carry out a 'blue light' transfer, but it did not arrive until 4.10pm. The ambulance waited at the MRI for 15 minutes and inexplicably was sent away again at 4.26pm. Not until 5.33pm did the MRI realise its mistake and call for another ambulance. Unbelievably this was also delayed an hour so that the claimant only reached the waiting neurosurgery team at 7.30pm. The operation was a success but he soon developed a post-operative intra-cranial infection (a common product of raised intra-cranial pressure). The damage done was considerable and it was determined that he would never work as a doctor again. He was suffering significant cognitive and neuropsychological deficit and Adjustment Disorder.

The Claimant brought a claim against the Defendant claiming damages for negligent delay. He further alleged delay in summonsing a 'blue light' ambulance for transfer to another hospital. He argued that had an earlier CT scan been carried out, he would have been transferred to the specialist neurosurgery team much earlier and surgery performed much sooner. In respect of causation, it was alleged that he had suffered an extended period of raised intra-cranial pressure, which itself materially contributed to the cognitive and neuropsychological deficits and Adjustment Disorder which resulted in him being unable to work as a Doctor.

The Defendant denied liability arguing that it was not open to the Claimant to rely upon the doctrine of material contribution as the post-operative infection operated both consecutively and concurrently to the Claimant's cognitive and neuropsychological deficits. Therefore, the Claimant could not rely upon *Bailey v The Ministry of Defence* [2008] EWCA Civ 883 as there were multiple causes of injury which occurred simultaneously. Rather it was a *Wilsher v Essex Area HA* [1988] 1 AC 1074 type case of multiple, possible causes and the Claimant could not prove causation. Defendant went on to argue that even if the Claimant succeeded on material contribution, he could only do so to the extent that the Defendant's negligence had materially contributed to the injury by using some sort of apportionment exercise.

The Claimant was successful. Mr Justice Picken concluded the following in respect of the doctrine of material contribution:

- The doctrine of material contribution can be relied upon in clinical negligence cases where there are multiple, causative agents which are both negligent and non-negligent. There is no support in the case law to suggest otherwise (para 95 of the judgment).

- *Wilsher* had been wrongly understood by the Defendant. Wilsher is not a barrier to Claimants succeeding in cases of multiple causes. Rather, Wilsher requires that Claimants prove, on a balance of probabilities, that an individual cause materially contributed to the injury. Possibility is not enough. Proof to the civil standard is required.

- Clinical negligence cases are different to industrial disease cases (para 97 of the judgment). Clinical negligence is concerned about material contribution to injury or damage and not about contribution to risk.

- Apportionment where material contribution is relied upon is wholly inappropriate (para 99 of the judgment) because the whole point of such cases is that medical science cannot quantify the various causative potencies of the causes.

- It doesn't really matter whether *Bailey* is a material contribution case or a classic, but for causation case. In similar cases, Claimants will succeed in recovering damages.

Cases on causation such as this are equally applicable to cosmetic surgery cases due to the nature of the surgery and complications that ensue. In *Williams v The Bermuda Hospitals Board*, [2016] UKPC 4 the court stated that a claimant must show that:

- The Defendant has been negligent in its care towards him.

- The negligence has materially contributed to his injury.

- Proving the degree of the contribution on a traditional *but for* basis is a medical impossibility, but the contribution must be more than minimal.

In such circumstances, the Claimant will recover damages in full in the case of an indivisible injury and in cases of divisible injury, damages for that part of the injury that was attributable to the Defendant's negligence.

Consider this against the 2013 case of Appleton and you may consider that that court erred in its ruling in Appleton. In Appleton v Medway NHS Foundation Trust [07/11/2013] when the claimant (who suffered from diabetes) and sought treatment when his foot became infected. Initial treatment was the provision of anti-biotics. When he re-attended, still infected, he was not provided with a broad-spectrum antibiotic, nor seen by a vascular surgeon, and was discharged. The next day he was admitted, but seen only by junior doctors. It was not until 3 days after admission that he was seen by a vascular surgeon who then arranged for a several toe amputations followed by the amputation of his lower leg. It was accepted that the failure to admit him and treat him via a vascular surgeon when he attended on the second occasion was negligent. It was alleged that the cause of the amputations was not the infection (which could have been treated better) but the underlying diabetes. The Judge concluded that there was insufficient evidence for the claimant to establish that the infection (which he found not to be a deep infection) caused (in the "material contribution" sense) the amputation.

These cases have an impact on cosmetic surgery cases where there are comorbidities which affect the claimant's recovery post operatively or if negligent delay contributes to the process of injury then if could be held to have made a material contribution. The Privy Council in *Williams v Bermuda Hospitals Board* [2016] UKPC4 determined when material contribution occurs where the events are sequential, and the issue of causation. It found that there is no distinction between simultaneous and consecutive cumulative causative factors i.e. where the injury is non-divisible. It found that delay had materially contributed to the Claimant's complications after surgery and that as a matter of principle, successive events are capable of each making a material contribution to the subsequent outcome.

CHAPTER EIGHT
CAUSATION

The Claimant must prove that the breach of duty complained of caused the injury complained of. **Chester v Afshar** [2004] UKHL 41 is an important case regarding causation. The House of Lords decided that a doctor's failure to fully inform a patient of all surgery risks vitiates the need to show that harm would have been caused by the failure to inform. Miss Chester was referred to Dr Afshar, a neurological expert, about some lower back pain. He told her that surgery was a solution, but (the judge found at first instance) did not inform her of the 1-2% risk of these operations going wrong. She suffered a complication, called cauda equina syndrome. The judge found that there was a causal connection between the failure to inform and Miss Chester's injuries – if she had been informed, she would have sought further advice or alternatives. In the Court of Appeal, Hale LJ, Sir Christopher Slade and Sir Denis Henry upheld the conclusion of the judge. A surgeon owes a general duty to a patient to warn him or her of possible serious risks involved in the procedure. Thus the courts started to depart from medical paternalism. A patient has a prima facie right to be informed by a surgeon of a small, but well-established, risk of serious injury as a result of surgery.

Establishing causation can be a difficult task. It must be demonstrated that 'but for' the doctor's action/inaction the harm complained of would not have occurred or that if a patient was informed of the risks, they would not have undertaken the procedure. Claims for negligence most frequently fail due to an inability to establish causation as there are often a variety of possible explanations for the outcome. However, if it can be shown that the breach materially contributed to the damage or it is more likely that the damage was due to negligence then that is usually sufficient.

Sometimes, in the absence of any other reasonable explanation for a phenomenon, the principle of 'res ipsa loquitur' (literally 'the thing speaks for itself') applies (e.g. leaving behind retained swab). Such a situation would apply to procedures performed on the wrong side or wrong type (e.g. breast reduction instead of enlargement). If damage occurs from that, then causation is assumed to be established unless the defendant can show that there is another reasonable explanation.

In *Crossman v St George's Healthcare NHS Trust* [2016] EWHC 2878 the claimant underwent a cervical laminectomy and foraminotomy for severe neck restriction and numbness in his left arm. Breach was admitted. The defendant placed the claimant on the waiting list for surgery after his first meeting with a consultant, at which it was agreed that his symptoms should first be treated using physiotherapy. It was also admitted that this error was not recognised or rectified. The Claimant was not informed that physiotherapy was still the recommended treatment, at the pre-operative assessment or when he was admitted to hospital the day before the surgery. The surgery was not negligently performed but he developed serious radicular nerve root injury. The risk of this occurring was agreed between the experts as 0.5-1%. It was agreed that had the claimant had the recommended physiotherapy, he would nevertheless have come to surgery around three months later than he in fact did.

The claimant was successful on the basis of "but for" causation. The Defendant had alleged contributory negligence (in failing to question the hospital's change of plan) and no medical causation (on the basis that the outcome, although statistically unlikely, was inevitable in any event for this patient).

The judge was reluctant to extend the principle of the right to informed choice from failure to warn of risks (as in Chester) to cases such as this one in which the risks had been properly explained but a late change of plan had not been. The Judge described this as "*a different and lesser category*" in which "*modification of the normal approach to causation would not be justified*".

In *Chantelle Pringle v Nestor Prime Care Services Ltd* [2014] EWCA 1308 (QB) the claimant, aged 2, was unwell with a high temperature, vomiting and other symptoms. Her mother telephoned her GP shortly after midnight and was passed to the Defendant's out of hours service. The triage nurse assessed the child as being 'lethargic' but advised that it was likely to be an upper respiratory tract infection and did not arrange for a home visit or admission to hospital. The child then developed a rash and was admitted to hospital the next morning and developed gangrene in both feet. The child had bilateral amputations. The claimant succeeded on causation in that medical science was not able to determine the crucial time by when treatment would have been effective but the delay materially contributed more than negligibly to the gangrene and amputation.

In *Julia Coakley v Dr Henrietta Rosie* [2014] EWHC 1790 (QB) the court considered the case of bacterial meningitis. The claimant claimed that 'but for' the Defendant's negligence, she would have avoided her injuries. The court held that the claimant was in the early stages of meningitis when she saw the defendant and that had she received treatment from the Defendant, she would have avoided injury. The judge concluded, that had the 'but for' test not succeeded, she would have succeeded in establishing that the delay materially contributed to the injuries.

CHAPTER NINE
DEFENCES

A medical treatment provider is able to defend a cosmetic surgery negligence claim where they can prove:

- They did not have a duty of care.
- The Claimant failed to establish a breach of any duty of care.
- Their conduct met the standard of care of a reasonable person.
- Failure to establish that the injury was caused by their breach.
- Failure to establish causation.
- A reasonable person could not have foreseen the damage suffered.
- Limitation expired and the matter is statute barred.
- Patient was fully informed of the risks and complications and consented to the same.
- Even if the risks and complications had been known and discussed the claimant would still have had the treatment complained of.

A 'duty of care' defence is extremely rare. A duty is deemed inherent within the relationship. More often the case will be fought on breach of duty and causation. The defendant will try and show it was 'more probable than not' that the breach did not cause the injury and any resultant loss. However, the High Court considered the extent of the duty of care owed to attending patients by receptionists in A&E departments in the case of *Darnley v Croydon Health Services* [2-15] EWHC 2301 (QB). The claimant attended A&E after sustaining a head injury in an assault. He booked in at reception and on his evidence had a severe headache, was feeling very drowsy and was finding it difficult to speak. Despite this he was not seen by triage with any urgency and was advised by the receptionist that he would have a four to five hour wait before being seen. After 20 minutes, he felt sufficiently unwell and unable to wait for several hours that he decided to go home. He then deteriorated at home and an ambulance was called. He had surgery to drain a haematoma on the brain and was left with significant brain injury and disability.

It was agreed between the parties that had he been triaged in hospital within 30 minutes (which should have happened) the severity of his condition would have been recognised and he would have undergone investigations and surgery earlier than occurred. The case turned on whether the reception staff should have arranged a priority triage and whether they were negligent in advising the claimant that he would have to wait four to five hours to be seen.

The court accepted that it was foreseeable, considering the lengthy waiting time that the claimant was given, that he would decide to go home. It was further accepted that had he been told he would be assessed within 30 minutes, that he would have waited, and that not being seen in this timescale could result in an adverse outcome for him. It was clear therefore that the receptionist had not managed the claimant properly and that it was foreseeable that the failures would lead to injury. The main question however was whether the reception staff owed any duty of care to the claimant and whether any liability arose from the failure to provide correct information about the waiting time.

Ultimately the court decided that it was not fair, just or reasonable to impose that duty of care and hold the hospital liable for the actions of the receptionist. It was held that provision of information about waiting times was not clinical information and there was no duty to be accurate about the information provided – even though that information might influence the actions or decisions of patients. The court also decided that there is no duty to guard patients against harm caused by them taking a decision not to wait to be seen.

Thus, the court decided that no liability rested with reception staff despite accepting that patients may rely on information they provide when making decisions which could have adverse consequences for their health. It is an interesting case which has implications for cosmetic surgery litigation as so much information is passed to patients from non-qualified staff who are not clinically trained, nor are they providing care. However, if they provide inaccurate information that has serious consequences, it seems unfair that there is no recourse for a claimant. The matter is being appealed and if it succeeds, it is likely to have a significant impact on non-qualified or receptionists not just in A&E but GP practices and cosmetic surgery clinics.

In addition, as we have seen, the concept of contributory negligence (i.e. that the patient has contributed to their loss and that the injury occurred as a result of the patient failing to take reasonable care for their health/safety) can be pleaded and the courts are willing to entertain the concept. In intentional torts, the defence operates in the form of consent. Where the claimant has consented to the defendant's act they will have no action. A patient who signs a consent form for a surgical operation cannot later sue the surgeon for battery. Where the harm was negligently inflicted, the defence gives rise to greater difficulties. The defendant has to show that the claimant assumed the legal risk of injury in circumstances where the defendant's act would otherwise amount to negligence. The effect of the defence is that the claimant consents to exempt the defendant from a duty of care which would otherwise have been owed.

The requirements for a defence of volenti non fit injuria mean that it must be shown that the claimant acted voluntarily in the sense that they could exercise a free choice. The claimant must have knowledge of the existence of the risk and its nature and extent. The test for knowledge is subjective. If the claimant should have been aware of the risk but was not, the defence will fail.

CHAPTER TEN
INJURY AND COMPENSATION

Women have reported serious and debilitating problems following cosmetic surgery treatment and the impact that even mild scarring or lumps can have is significant. Although the number of reports to MHRA is low compared to the overall use of cosmetic treatments, there is some evidence of under-reporting and there are concerns that MHRA is not aware of all women who have experienced problems with fillers, Botox or implants.

It is difficult to give an indication as to the value of a claim until it is fully investigated and relevant medical evidence obtained. Compensatory damages are split into two areas – '*General*' and '*Special*'. The legal basis for assessing damages is clear in that so far as financially possible, the claimant should be put back into the position as if the negligence had not occurred. In terms of pecuniary loss, the fundamental principle is that he claimant is entitled to full compensation i.e. 100% of the value of his or her proven net expenses and losses.

The claimant is under a duty to take reasonable steps to mitigate his or her loss. The burden is on the Defendant to prove that the claimant has failed to do so. In *Totham v King's College Hospitals NHS Foundation Trust* [2015] EWHC 97 (QB) the defendant challenged past case management fees on the basis that they significantly exceeded the estimate. The court rejected the argument stating that the claimant's mother had taken care to appoint a reputable company, had changed case managers and checked whether their fees were out of line.

Whether or not heads of future expenses are recoverable is again due to reasonableness. Claimants are entitled to damages to meet their reasonable requirements or needs arising from their injuries (*Sowden v Lodge* (2004) EWCA Civ 1370).

General Damages

General Damages are for pain, suffering and loss of amenity, both in the past and future including any surgery that may be needed connected to the negligence. It is based on the age of the claimant at the time of surgery and whether the injury is permanent and if so, what the level of disability is. How long is the injury expected to last? It the injury site to the face? Does it involve genital cosmetic surgery and if so what are the long-term consequences? Psychological harm is an important consideration for most claimants.

Obtain a report from a Consultant in the same discipline as the cosmetic procedure. Additional reports from Consultant Psychiatrist / psychologist will identify any recognised condition and recommend treatment if applicable. If there is significant scarring then get a report detailing what, if any, treatment can be administered to improve the appearance. There may be surgical or cover up makeup as an option.

Always send the GMC guidance on consent to the expert and ask that they refer to the specific provisions when preparing the report to show evidence or lack thereof of the provisions.

It is important to consider the range of injuries when looking at a cosmetic surgery case. Injuries can be wide ranging and initially a claimant may just feel that something is wrong without fully understanding what and why. The injuries will also determine the number and types of reports needed. A few are set out here by way of illustration.

Genital Cosmetic Surgery

Demand for cosmetic genital surgery (genitoplasty) is increasing and the number of labial reductions in the NHS has doubled in the past five years. Vaginoplasty is a procedure that aims to 'tighten up' the vagina which may have become loose from vaginal childbirth or aging. Some clinics claim it can improve sensitivity which is strongly challenged. While it's true that vaginal tissues can stretch, surgically tightening the vaginal tissue cannot guarantee a heightened sexual response. It has been shown that desire, arousal, and orgasm are complex, highly personal responses, based on emotional and interpersonal factors rather than aesthetic ones. In addition, sexual "sensitivity" doesn't automatically lead to more pleasure but rather it can lead to pain and significant life-long pain.

Labiaplasty (the skin surrounding the vagina) can be performed alone or with vaginoplasty. Surgery can be performed on the labia major (the larger, outer vaginal lips), or the labia minor (the smaller, inner vaginal lips). Labiaplasty changes the size or shape of the labia, typically making them smaller or correcting an asymmetry between them. Vaginal rejuvination procedures claim to increase sensitivity and tighten (by burning with a laser and creating scar tissue) whilst also curing incontinence issues. Procedures to restore the hymen, unhood the clitoris and amplify the G-shot using collage are all being developed and sold. They can cause irreparable damage. The injuries sustained during genital cosmetic surgery are varied but consistent. The list is not mutually exclusive; more than one complication may be experienced.

- Pain – includes post-operative pain and ongoing pain on standing, walking or during intercourse.
- Extrusion/erosion – refers to incidents where mesh used has either migrated or become partially exposed through vaginal tissue.
- Infection e.g. any recurring urinary tract infections or discharge (some infections are so recurrent that constant antibiotics creates new problems. Eventually the scope of antibiotics available becomes limited.
- Relapse of conditions/urinary symptoms – reoccurrence of urinary incontinence in laser rejuvenation treatment.
- Scarring.
- Loss of sensitivity.
- Stretching leading to tearing.
- Perforation of organ – refers to incidents that were procedural related, such as perforation of the bladder or bowel.
- Sexual difficulties – dyspareunia, painful sexual intercourse leading to abstinence.

- Fistulas.
- Psychological injury.

There have been three incidents reported to MHRA where the patient died after surgery for vaginal mesh implant insertion to treat SUI. All were reported by healthcare professionals in England. For all three cases, there was agreement with the healthcare professionals who reported that the reported complications: bowel perforation and cardiac episode were consistent with complications related to the surgical procedure itself and that the mesh implant was not implicated as the cause of death. All surgery has risks and underlying health conditions or other factors may also contribute to complications, including death when under general anaesthetic.

Breast Augmentation and Implants

In relation to breast augmentation, look for issues such as:

- Bleeding into the breast tissues causing swollen, painful breasts.
- Infection resulting in unsightly scarring.
- Reduction or loss of nipple sensation.
- Lumps (but not cysts).
- Pain under the arm or in the armpit.
- For implants that have ruptured – silicone in the lymph nodes in sufficient quantity to amount to injury.
- Hardening of the breast following rupture.
- Rippling.
- The breast feeling hot.

- Psychiatric injury attributable to the breast injury.
- Pain.
- Denting, softening or other significant changes in breast shape.
- Bottoming out - were the implant falls under the breast line (likewise when the skin attached to the breast bone comes away and gives the appearance of one large breast.

The majority of silicone gel breast implant ruptures are 'silent' e.g. no definitive diagnosis can be made as the silicone gel stays in the 'pocket' which is the space surrounding the breast implant and the breast does not appear deflated. Thus, the Claimant should have an MRI scan (magnetic resonance imaging) to detect a rupture.

The FDA recommend that all patients be informed by their cosmetic surgeon that they should obtain an MRI scan 3 years after augmentation and then every 2 years thereafter in order to detect any silent rupture. The implants can then be removed and replaced before any long-term issues with silicone can occur. They also require mammograms yearly at age 40 and every year thereafter to detect breast cancer. There is not the same requirement in the UK at present.

For a saline implant, any rupture would be detected very quickly say within hours or days. It tends to flatten very quickly if there is an opening in it. If the valve is leaking it will be slower to deflate.

Capsular contracture is a naturally occurring problem which can occur when the body rejects the breast implants. This can occur with any breast implants at any time and can lead to surgeons recommending that the implants are replaced. If the claimant is diagnosed with capsular contracture the case is unlikely to be actionable per se but the subsequent management may be.

Rhinoplasty

Those seeking a rhinoplasty may be seeking a straighter nose, refined shorter tip, a curve, widening nostrils to aid breathing, to create even nostrils, correcting bends in the nose etc. For a primary rhinoplasty between 5-10% require revision surgery. Following surgery, the nose will continue to change for up to 1 year and thus there may still be improvements. Non-surgical rhinoplasty (fillers in the nose) can have untoward complications for a variety of reasons. As the nose has a sensitive blood supply it can be compromised when using fillers if not performed correctly. Fillers are a poor option for lengthening the nose.

In *Zahir v Vadodaria* [2016] EWHC 1215 (QB) Mr Shailesh Vadodaria carried out a rhinoplasty operation on Mrs Mijin Zahir at Highgate Hospital in London. From the time she came around from the anaesthetic after that operation, Mrs Zahir was unhappy with the resulting appearance of her nose. Revision surgery was conducted by Mr Vadodaria on 23 June 2011, but Mrs Zahir remained dissatisfied. She has subsequently undergone three further operations, these conducted by a second plastic surgeon. The Judge said that the 'experts had considered the wrong question when addressing whether the outcome was satisfactory. The key question was whether the surgical technique used was acceptable'. The claim failed.

Lasers and IPL

Laser hair removal is the process of removing unwanted hair via pulsed light, which destroys hair follicles over a period of time. Several sessions are necessary as hair grows in phases and therefore treatment is needed at the appropriate hair-growth stage. Once it has been agreed that treatment will take place and appropriate consent has been taken, a patch test will need to take place. This will be a small area of the skin that will be given some treatment to see how it reacts to the laser over a period of days before a session of treatments is started. The complications associated with use of lasers and IPL in the treatment of skin conditions, including hair reduction, are:

- Damage to the eye and vision such as corneal abrasions, retinal burns, damage to blood vessels in the eye, and macular damage (opaque spots on the cornea) which can result in total blindness.
- Injury to the skin such as scarring, hyperpigmentation (darkening of pigmentation), hypo and depigmentation (loss of pigment resulting in pale or white areas), burns and blisters, infection, bruising, prolonged redness, and milia (tiny cysts).
- Worsening of pre-existing skin conditions such as acne or rosacea.

Prior to October 2010, the use of Intense Pulse Lasers (IPL) and lasers for cosmetic purposes was regulated by the Care Quality Commission (CQC). On 1 October 2010, the use of IPL was deregulated. Since then there has been an influx of therapists, not all appropriately trained. A practitioner should have a minimum of an NVQ3 or equivalent.

There are a number of conditions which are contra-indicative for laser hair removal. It is advisable for a patient to have consulted their GP if any of these are concerns but they usually don't. A common cause for excess body hair (hirsutism) is polycystic ovarian syndrome (PCOS), and any underlying health issues need to be ruled out. The clinic should advise the patient to seek medical advice before going ahead with the treatment.

The degree of damage and the location of the injury will affect the value of the claim. Common areas for treatment for both men and women include arms, legs, bikini line, armpits, upper lip and chin. A laser hair removal claim is likely to come under Judicial College Guidelines 'scarring to other parts of the body'. There is a wide range of values for burns particularly if they lead to ongoing physical or psychological injuries.

Determine firstly

- the percentage body area affected by the burns;

- whether the burns are full thickness, partial thickness or superficial;
- the cosmetic impact of the injury and the injured person's reactions to them;
- the need for (and extent of) surgery;
- any resulting disability;
- the psychological impact.

The Judicial College Guidelines also highlights the fact that where there is a cosmetic element, the courts have drawn a distinction between levels of damages for males and females. Awards vary from £40,600 to £81,000 at the top end of the scale for women to £24,000 to £55,000 for men. At the other end of the scale, where the effect of scarring is minor, the award will be between £1,430 to £2,940 for both genders. In *NB v JC* (2015) the claimant succeeded on liability and received £3,500 (out of court settlement) for injuries caused by negligent IPL laser hair removal. She suffered superficial burns to her arms, peeling and dyspigmentation which resolved in 3-4 months. The burns were painful and obvious and affected her confidence but no psychiatric claim was made.

Liposuction

Liposuction is one of the most popular procedures currently performed. Liposuction is not primarily a weight loss option. It is a body contouring procedure and therefore the inherent limitation and safety issues must be highlighted. It is associated with a variety of complications for instance:

- Oedema and ecchymosis – swelling and oedema occurs in almost every liposuction procedure as a normal reaction of the human issues. It is controlled by wearing a compression garment for about 4-6 weeks. Post operative oedema with unusual pain beyond this may be due to excessive trauma leading to an internal burn-like injury This will take longer to settle and may result in increased scarring, fibrosis and contour irregularities. If it persists it can be related to pre-operative anaemia, reduced serum proteins and kidney malfunction.

- Focal Excessive Liposuction is the removal of an excessive amount of fat from a localized area of the body. Removing too much fat can have an unnatural and unattractive appearance. If uneven or irregular excessive liposuction of a single area occurs, it produces depressions (lipotrops) or lumps and bumps (liponots. It is not the goal to remove the maximum amount of fat. It is the right level of fat that remains after liposuction that determines success.

- Full Thickness Skin Necrosis (death of the affected skin) can result from excessive superficial liposuction that injures the vascular supply of the overlying skin.

- Erythema Ab Liporaspiration is a permanent blotchy (net-like pattern) pink-brown discoloration of the skin resulting from rasping the undersurface of the skin during superficial liposuction.

- The manufacturer of Reston foam, 3M Corp., has warned against the use of Reston foam for liposuction. Reston foam is not intended to be applied to patients' skin. An allergic reaction to the adhesive on the foam (similar to an allergic reaction to poison oak or poison ivy) can cause blisters and an increased risk of necrotizing fasciitis, a potentially lethal infection

It is believed that an unwanted side effect is that it makes other parts of the body fatter. Although the fat will not return to the areas of the body where it was removed from, it will reappear elsewhere such as the shoulders and arms. The procedure usually costs up to £5,000.

Dental

Like any dental surgery, cosmetic dental implant surgery poses complications and risks. Risks include:

- Infection at the implant site.
- Injury or damage to surrounding structures, such as other teeth or blood vessels.
- Nerve damage, which can cause pain, numbness or tingling in your natural teeth, gums, lips or chin.
- Sinus problems, when dental implants placed in the upper jaw protrude into one of your sinus cavities.

In *Clamp v K* (2015) the claimant recovered an out of court settlement for PSLA of £60,000 for dental injuries and resulting symptoms suffered such as prolonged pain, difficulty eating and speaking for four-and-a-half years, numbness to her lips, sinusitis and an adjustment disorder. The Claimant alleged that the defendant was negligent in inadequately planning and assessing the treatment, using poor surgical skills during the procedures and placing crowns and bridgework in her mouth which were of an unacceptable standard. The claimant would need treatment in the future and was advised to have cognitive behavioural treatment.

Derma Fillers

The complications associated with the injection of dermal fillers include:

- Infection: acute or chronic leading to unsightly scarring.
- Lumpiness: firm, raised nodules.

- Granuloma formation: a type of tissue reaction resulting in lumps and nodules in the skin which can be chronic and may be related to progressive destruction and deformity.
- Ulcer formation: break down of the overlying skin resulting in an open sore.
- Vascular occlusion: blockage of a blood vessel.
- Tissue necrosis (tissue death): occurs when the blood supply to the skin and tissues is compromised, and results in loss of the affected tissues.
- Allergic reaction: redness, swelling and discomfort in the area injected or systemic allergic response.
- Prolonged swelling, bruising: significant swelling and bruising of the tissue which can be difficult to disguise.
- Blindness: this complication is rare but has been associated with a range of filler injections used in the periorbital area (area around the eyes).

In *Kathleen Webster & Ors v Mark Liddington & Ors* [2014] EWCA Civ 560 the Court of Appeal had to consider, whether clinicians were responsible for statements in a manufacturer's brochure for skin rejuvenation treatment, which they had passed on to prospective patients without a disclaimer. The court considered what a reasonable person in the patient's position would understand from the clinician's words or infer from the clinicians conduct and all the circumstances. The Court held that 'a reasonable person standing in the shoes of any of the claimants would conclude on the facts that the clinician was adopting the manufacturer's brochure's contents'.

Special Damages

Special Damages are other financial losses that can consist of:

- Past and future care
- Past and future loss of earnings
- Loss of pension
- Equipment and home adaptations
- Costs of counselling
- Costs of corrective surgery/physiotherapy
- Travel Expenses
- Specialist clothing or makeup

Future loss of earnings is by far the highest award. Such awards can run into several thousands of pounds. Where the cosmetic surgery negligence is debilitating, the claimant may well have to give up their career. In some cases of genital surgery, the claimant is unable to walk far and there have been tragic cases where the Claimant has to give up work and has been confined to a wheel chair. Whilst this is an extreme example of surgery gone wrong, you cannot under estimate the impact that surgery gone wrong has on the claimant. Thus, it is important to meet with the client and find out how the surgery has impacted on their lives to offer them the best coordinated representation.

CHAPTER ELEVEN MEDICAL DEVICES REGULATION

The Medicines and Healthcare Products Regulatory Agency (MHRA)

The Medicines and Healthcare Products Regulatory Agency regulates medicines, medical devices and blood components for transfusion in the UK. MHRA is an executive agency, sponsored by the Department of Health and manages the operation of the European Union regulatory system for medical devices within the UK. The role of MHRA, as the UK CA, is to ensure that all medical devices placed on the UK market are compliant with the relevant legislation and to enforce this legislation on behalf of the Secretary of State.

MHRA is responsible for overseeing the activities and ongoing designation of notified bodies within the UK and for operating the UK medical device vigilance system. Safety of medical devices is dependent on the collaborative actions of several key stakeholders, including manufacturers, notified bodies, healthcare professionals and patients themselves.

Primarily the manufacturer is responsible for the safety and performance of the device. For some higher risk devices, notified bodies (designated and monitored by the MHRA) will assess the manufacturer's quality system and sample the technical and clinical data before the device is placed on the market. However, the role of the MHRA in assessing the safety of devices in use is mostly post-market. If the MHRA confirms that an implant is dangerous to health and instigates a recall, it would be likely that a product liability claim against a manufacturer would follow. Evidence available to the MHRA on the safety of implants is based on various sources including, adverse incident reports, published peer reviewed literature and information from implant manufacturers, patients and healthcare professionals.

There is no single database that records how many implants are implanted or removed within the UK. The Health and Social Care Information Centre runs the Health Episodes Statistics (HES) database to record details of all admissions, outpatient appointments and A&E

attendances at NHS hospitals in England. HES data are a useful indicator of how many operations take place in England. It is essentially limited to demographic, diagnostic and procedural information, and requires careful interpretation. There is no obligation to record private hospital data.

The MHRA supports familiarity with existing NICE and professional guidance on the safe and appropriate use of implants. It states that the pertinent NICE guidelines should be followed for surgical procedures with regards to patient consent, audit, adverse event reporting to MHRA and specialist care for certain surgery.

Where there is an issue with an implant or medicine, the Yellow Card Scheme is vital in helping the MHRA monitor the safety of all healthcare products in the UK to ensure they are acceptably safe for patients and those that use them. Reports can be made for all medicines including vaccines, blood factors and immunoglobulins, herbal medicines and homeopathic remedies, and all medical devices available on the UK market. From the 20th of May 2016, the MHRA is also collecting reports of safety concerns associated with e-cigarette products through the Yellow Card Scheme.

It is worth considering making a report if your client has a suspected problem or incident involving

- side effects (also known as adverse drug reactions or ADRs);
- medical device adverse incidents;
- defective medicines (those that are not of an acceptable quality);
- counterfeit or fake medicines or medical devices.

By reporting adverse incidents, it is helping to build a picture to identify issues which might not have been previously known about. The MHRA will review the product if necessary, and take action to minimise risk and maximise benefit to the patients. The MHRA is also able to investigate counterfeit or fake medicines or devices and if necessary protect public health with appropriate action.

All medicines can cause side effects but those reported on the Yellow Card are evaluated, together with additional sources of information such as clinical trial data, medical literature or data from international medicines regulators, to identify previously unknown safety issues. Safety experts assess the reports. They are made up of doctors, pharmacists and scientists who study the benefits and risks of medicines. If a new side effect is identified, the safety profile of the medicine in question is carefully looked at, as well as the side effects of other medicines used to treat the same condition.

The basis for the current view held by the MHRA is in part due to the reporting of adverse incidents. With lack of reports about implants, the feeling is that most if not all risks and complications stem from clinical practice rather than an inherent defect in implants. Increased reporting in future may alter this perception as more studies will be carried out into the suitability of say, silicone as an implant medium. The MHRA is attempting to encourage more clinicians, patients, hospitals, and manufacturers to report adverse incidents.

Ongoing research projects are likely to provide useful information about the long-term safety and effectiveness of silicone implant devices to meet essential requirements, including biocompatibility, toxicity, technical specifications, clinical data, sterilisation, right through to packaging and labelling.

Manufacturers must also ensure that any declared benefits of their devices outweigh the risks. Failure to do so may result in a range of options from prosecution where there is a serious risk to public health, or for repeated non-compliance, to other forms of less noticeable compliance action where the product may remain on the market pending the corrective action. MHRA can also enforce suspension notices and prohibition notices to restrict, suspend or stop the supply of any device which is unsafe or not in compliance with the Regulations.

The EU has a process that allows individual Competent Authorities (CA) to share details of identified compliance issues with other member states. This communication is shared on the understanding that information will be kept confidential, in accordance with EU legislation. Once products are CE marked (the manufacturer declares that the product conforms with the relevant essential requirements in the relevant Medical Device Directive (MDD) and is fit for its intended purpose as specified by the manufacturer) they can be placed across the EU without further restrictions.

A medical device with a CE mark indicates that the manufacturer has made a 'declaration of conformity' that their product meets the relevant essential requirements that apply. This would include demonstrating that the following are satisfactory:

- the benefits outweigh any risks;
- clinical evaluation;
- biological/toxicological safety data;
- sterilization validation data.

When an adverse incident is reported to the MHRA, even if there is a lack of verifiable evidence, the MHRA treats these incidents seriously and all reports are kept on record should further scientific or clinical evidence emerge. Every adverse incident reported to the MHRA from a patient or member of the public is passed on to the manufacturer of the device concerned for the manufacturer to conduct further investigation and to contribute to their post-market surveillance, which is required under the MDD. Members of the public have the option to only allow the device details and the account of the adverse event to be given to the manufacturer. Personal details will only be sent if the member of the public has given consent for this.

If any of these adverse incident reports are subsequently determined to be vigilance reportable under the MDD, then the manufacturer is required to inform MHRA, carry out an investigation as appropriate, send a report with their conclusion and root cause analysis.

Evidence from other Regulators

It is important to consider whether manufacturing defects and recalls are being considered by other regulators in other countries. This may impact in the UK and mirror problems encountered by patients here.

European Competent Authorities (CA)

Check whether there has been any evidence from other European CAs of problems or issues with certain implants. For instance, vaginal mesh implants were first discussed, in April 2012, at one of the regular monthly medical device vigilance teleconferences held with other European CAs. In another instance, in 2007 the MHRA referred concerns about PIP's handling of adverse incidents to the German notified body with responsibility for assessing PIP – TUV Rheinland – and was reassured by that body that they had 'looked into' these concerns, leading PIP to improve their practices.

Worldwide Regulators

The US Food and Drug Administration (FDA) and the Australian Therapeutic Goods Administration (TGA) have monitored actions and statements and guidance issued by other CAs. The US has produced several notifications and guidance on breast implants in the past. It is worth checking their website if a client complains about an 'implant'. They are usually ahead of the MHRA with regards to notifications of concern and you can determine if an implant manufacturer is causing concern.

Notified Bodies

Medical devices are certified by independent conformity assessment organisations called notified bodies. MHRA is the CA in the UK that oversees UK notified bodies. There are about 60 notified bodies designated across Europe that manufacturers may use, with five in the UK.

In September 2013, the European Commission (EC), under the current MDD, introduced a process of joint audit of notified bodies by multinational teams, replacing the previous system that left responsibility for the oversight of notified bodies solely to the competent authority of the Member State in which the notified body was based. This was introduced as a measure to ensure that all notified bodies were managed to harmonised standards across the EU. Thus, if there was a concern highlighted in another member state, the UK would be involved immediately to alert clinicians and manufacturers. How this will work post-Brexit remains to be seen.

Risk Assessment by Manufacturers

The first step for the manufacturer of a medical device is to follow the guidance set out by the EC guidance on clinical evaluation. This involves an analysis of the benefits and risks. A review of the intended benefits, potential harms and the potential sources of harm. Once the harms and sources have been identified, then they can be assessed to evaluate the risks. Are the risks as low as reasonably practical? Once all mitigating factors are in place, are the residual risks acceptable?

Manufacturers are required to make judgments relating to safety of their medical devices. Any risks or complications can be highlighted in the guidance literature and protected against by training clinicians. The acceptability of risks accounts is the measure of potential risk, in order to determine its suitability to be placed on the market for its intended use.

Manufacturers are also required to undertake post-market surveillance activities to review experience of their devices in use and then implement any necessary corrective actions as a result of their review. Such safety corrective actions will need to be notified to CAs and to device users through a Field Safety Notice. A manufacturer should review the risk-benefit analysis in light of data gathered in the post-market phase.

The notified body will carry out an audit of the manufacturer's full quality assurance system in accordance to the internationally agreed standard on quality assurance for medical devices (ISO 13485) and the requirements of the relevant conformity annex of the Directive. The review of the technical file covers as a minimum:

- the intended use of the device;
- the validity of the essential requirements checklist;
- a review of the risk management file (which would comprise a thorough review of the clinical evaluation report and the risk–benefit analysis);
- pre-clinical data (studies in animal models, biocompatibility, technical performance tests etc.);
- clinical evaluation in accordance with Annex X of the MDD (93/42/EEC);
- information supplied by the manufacturer in the labelling and instructions;
- other technical documentation based on risk.

The sampling regimen for technical files is set out by the European Operations Group for notified bodies. At least one product from each device group will be reviewed on a three-year cycle. Notified bodies are also required to review the appropriateness of the manufacturer's post-market surveillance system. In addition, the notified body is required to be provided with vigilance reports from the manufacturer when they are submitted to the relevant CA. These are reviewed to determine any significant or recurring issues. Where significant or recurring issues are noted, this could lead to an unannounced audit at the manufacturer's premises (such as with the PIP Implants). During audits of notified bodies, the CA will review the systems and processes in place to review and monitor vigilance reports. Examples of reports received will be reviewed and any action taken followed through. On certificate renewal and at onsite audits, the notified body will follow up on post-market data to ensure this is being collected and that the manufacturer's procedures relating to risk are still in line with the requirements. Technical files will continue to be reviewed in accordance to the sampling regime described above. Visits can be brought forward if the device in question is frequently non-compliant or if specific information provides reasons to suspect non-conformities of the devices or of their manufacturer.

In the Poly Implant Prothèse (PIP) incident, the French company that produced silicone gel breast implants were subject to several unannounced visits. They were found to have been illegally manufacturing and selling breast implants made from cheaper industrial-grade silicone since 2001 (instead of the mandated medical-grade silicone they had previously used). The hundreds of thousands of unapproved implants sold globally by PIP from 2001 to 2010 were found to have a 500% higher risk of rupturing or leaking than approved models, as well as being implicated in at least several deaths due to systemic toxicity and several cases of induced breast cancer. The scandal produced fears of a massive health disaster and one which will only be fully revealed over time. A full recall of the company's implants by the French health ministry in 2010 lead to thousands of women in the UK seeking removal and in many instances replacement.

Thus, for solicitors bringing claims there is substantive guidance and safety information available to use in evidence. However, the application of the existing medical devices directives has been inconsistent across the EU which makes it difficult for the legislation to achieve its objectives. Moreover, the regulatory framework is under scrutiny following the safety concerns of some metal-on-metal hip replacements and fraudulent PIP breast implants.

The MHRA has engaged with the European Commission to influence its proposals as they develop. The main features of the regulations that have been proposed include:

- increasing transparency;

- increasing requirements on traceability in the supply chain;
- tightening up the designation and audit of notified bodies, which assess the safety of devices before they are placed on the market;
- subjecting higher risk devices to additional pre-market scrutiny;
- requiring more clinical evidence for higher risk and implantable devices;
- introducing reporting of serious incidents and field safety corrective actions to a new central EU database;
- improving coordination between Member States;
- establishing a new governance structure of Member State experts and centralised clinical expertise; and;
- aligning with the EU's recently updated New Legislative Framework for the internal market.

It is expected that new legislation will be in place in 2018 and from then all products on the market in the UK will need to comply with the new rules. However, these new rules will not be applied retrospectively, therefore existing products will not need to be updated to meet the new requirements. How this will be implemented post-Brexit is unknown.

Traceability and Unique Device Identifiers (UDIs)

One of the major innovations of the proposed regulations is to establish a system of unique device identification (UDI). These precise codes placed on every medical device by the manufacturer, linked to a database that holds detailed information on all devices. UDI will facilitate the identification and traceability of devices. Economic operators and health institutions will be obliged to maintain electronic records of UDIs and manufacturers will be required to refer to the UDI in their technical documentation, when reporting serious incidents and undertaking field safety corrective actions.

Implementation of the UDI system will be proportionate and risk-based. The proposed regulations for medical devices will require manufacturers of implantable devices to provide an implant card for patients. The regulation sets out what information needs to be included on the card (in plain language):

- the UDI code,
- any relevant warnings,
- the expected lifetime of the device and
- any follow-up of which the patient should be aware.

This is a development which flows from the requirements of informed consent and patient autonomy to provide patients with as much information as possible. It became clear during the events involving fraudulent PIP breast implants that many patients did not know the manufacturer of their breast implants. Implant cards will improve traceability and patients' awareness. UDI's will help to monitor the safety and performance of implantable medical devices.

European Scientific Committee on Emerging and Newly Identified Health Risks

The European Commission can ask its independent Scientific Committee on Emerging and Newly Identified Health Risks (SCENIHR) to assess the health risks linked to the use of implants or devices if issues are raised. Research is carried out to ascertain risks and safety of products. SCENIHR's recommendations can include:

- Material properties, product design, overall size, route of implantation, patient characteristics, associated procedures and surgeon's experience are aspects to consider when choosing appropriate therapy.

- A certification system for surgeons should be introduced based on existing international guidelines and established in cooperation with the relevant European Surgical Associations.

- Assessment of the risks reported for further report.

- Appropriate patient selection and counselling is extremely important for the optimal outcome for all surgical procedures.

What is interesting about the SCENIHR recommendations is that they did not seek to recommend the removal of intact PIP Implants as a matter of course, despite identifying that PIP silicone breast implants have far higher rupture rates than breast implants by other manufacturers. They found that 'no increased health risk has been associated with exposure to silicone gel emanating from a ruptured PIP implant, as compared with a conventional implant from another manufacturer'. There were no convincing medical, toxicological or other data to justify routine removal of intact PIP implants. However, 'the decision to remove an intact PIP implant for this reason should be based on an individual assessment of the woman's condition by her surgeon or other treating physician after consultation'.

Thus, it is a good source of information regarding implants and devices but should be closely monitored for updates.

CHAPTER TWELVE
GROSS NEGLIGENCE MANSLAUGHTER AND WILFUL NEGLECT

Gross Negligence Manslaughter

It is rare for a patient to die because of cosmetic surgery nevertheless it occurs. Coroners and police are more likely to consider whether a criminal act has taken place, allow an investigation and possibly laying charges of 'gross negligence manslaughter'. The increasing criminalisation of negligent healthcare professionals should not be ignored. The decision to press charges is determined by advice from the Special Crime and Counter Terrorism Division of the CPS. Although a complex decision making process, the test laid down in *R v Adomako* assists. The House of Lords stated that 'the test should be whether Dr Adomako's conduct and breach of care was 'so bad in all the circumstances ... as to constitute a crime'. Recklessness has been used to define 'gross negligence' in that the wrongdoer has an awareness of the consequences of an action, inaction or omission, but continues regardless.

In *R v Adomako* (1995) 1 AC 171 the defendant anaesthetist failed to notice for six minutes during the operation that the oxygen supply to the patient had become disconnected from the ventilator. The patient suffered a cardiac arrest and died. The House of Lords affirmed the conviction, and the elements of the offence were specified as:

- The defendant owed the victim a duty of care.
- The defendant breached that duty.
- The breach caused (or significantly contributed to) the victim's death.
- The breach was grossly negligent.

An individual cannot rely on hospital system failures in their defence. It is the standard of care given by the individual involved which is considered. Thus, doctors specialising in surgery, anaesthesia and obstetrics are vulnerable to prosecution. As there is an increase in cosmetic surgeries, there is increased likelihood of risk. In turn a greater number of prosecutions for GNM becomes likely.

Wilful Neglect or Ill Treatment

From April 2015, Section 20 of the Criminal Justice and Courts Act 2015 applies to individuals such as doctors and nurses and states that 'it is an offence for an individual who has the care of another individual by virtue of being a care worker to ill-treat or wilfully to neglect that individual'. The offence focuses on the conduct of the individual, not the outcome. It is to do with what the healthcare worker did or failed to do to the patient, rather than the harm that resulted.

It applies to organisations and individuals and thus clinics, hospitals and doctors in the cosmetic surgery sector need to be aware of their responsibilities. There needs to be a significant or serious departure from acceptable standards of care for there to be an offence in the cosmetic surgery setting.

CHAPTER THIRTEEN POTENTIAL SOURCES OF FUTURE HARM

Aside from individual clinical negligence instances in cosmetic surgery, future litigation for mass torts is likely to arise in the future given the expanding remit of cosmetic procedures. For breast or other implants (calf, pectoral, penile, testicular) against a manufacturer the claims will be based on an inherent flaw in the design or manufacture of the product that was known about at the time of manufacture. The longer an implant is in situ the more noticeable become the complications and more data becomes available about adverse incidents as they are reported. Future considerations are set out below.

The Material

Some devices are made of polypropylene, which is a polymer widely used in medical applications such as non-absorbable synthetic suture materials and in the repair of abdominal wall hernias. There is no current evidence to suggest that the use of this material in medical devices causes undue toxicological risk to patients. NICE guidance indicates that polypropylene is widely understood to be an inert material and when used as an implantable material generally elicits minimal host response. However, it does have a propensity to erode through vaginal mucosa and there can be failure of the vagina to heal over the mesh. It is also greatly dependent on the source material complying with health and medical regulations to ensure that it is medical grade and kept contamination free. Only time will tell if it remains a suitable material for surgical procedures.

Patient Related Factors

Factors that can be associated with surgical failures include, for example:

- smoking nicotine and e-cigarettes;

- BMI higher than 35;
- primary surgery vs secoplications such as dry eyes and night vision problems as a result of laser eye surgery. Some experience corneal neuropathic disease which is painful and unrelenting. Many experience dry eyes and sensitivitndary surgery;
- pre-operative anticholinergic medication use.

Patients may have several other comorbidities which could affect the outcome of surgery, while others may have none at all. Obese patients pose a challenge for cosmetic surgery. They are 12 times more likely to suffer a potentially deadly complication. They have a higher rate of post-operative complications such as heart failure, wound infection, nerve injury and urinary tract infections.

Laser Eye Surgery Complications

Alarming numbers of patients are experiencing comy to evaporation, wind or dry environments that exacerbates classic dry eye and increases neuralgia. Patients report severe, unremitting, burning pain and photophobia.

Patients have to apply eye drops daily – which in itself is a problem, as - long-term use can raise the risk of chronic eye inflammation. Dry eyes can also lead to serious infections and, ultimately, even loss of vision. Patients also experience 'floaters' which are black lines or dots that appear in the line of sight. Poor night vision is also reported.

There is no law preventing any surgeon from operating as an 'eye expert' — though the after a surgeon has demonstrated expertise in laser eye surgery. It recommends patients choose a surgeon with a minimum of three months' formal training in laser eye surgery who performs at least 500 eye laser operations a year.

How the Implant Is Used

There are surgical risks associated with implant procedures and these will vary according to which procedure is used and the final anatomical outcome. Surgical and procedural risk factors will include those mentioned in the manufacturer's instructions. The knowledge, experience, skills and training of the surgeon are also a significant factor. NICE guidelines say that surgeons should have experience for each type of procedure. Experience of using particular devices with some procedures is recommended as requiring higher levels of clinical governance and audit. Surgeons would be expected to take the manufacturers IFUs for the devices into account.

As with all surgical procedures, there is a developing level of expertise as the clinical community gains experience with the implantation of a particular device. This should be viewed against a background of understanding that the basic tenets of surgery remain across all of surgical practice so that although a component of the surgery may be new, the principles of surgical technique are essentially the same.

The Instructions for Use (IFU)

Further hazards could arise where instructions for use are inadequate or do not keep up to date with information gained in the post-market phase. Further work needs to be done to characterise long-term safety in relation to different surgical procedures such as genital cosmetic surgery.

Is There Cancer Risk?

This is a question which has been raised during the PIP Implant litigation and which creates a huge amount of concern and worry for patients. Despite long term studies supporting the efficacy and safety of macroporous, monofilament polypropylene slings, there have been concerns regarding the general risks of using mesh in transvaginal surgery. Recently some concerns about synthetic midurethral slings and a possible link with malignancy have arisen. Experiments in mice have demonstrated a high rate of sarcoma formation after implantation of polypropylene. However, further investigation suggests that the risk of malignancy may be related to surface area and morphology of the implanted material more than the material composition itself.

A study took place to examine any association between polypropylene mesh used in midurethral slings and malignancy in humans. A retrospective review was performed for all slings performed from 2004 to 2013. From within this group, urethral cancer, vaginal cancer and bladder cancer were reviewed. Then each case associated with malignancy was further examined. The rate of bladder cancer after sling procedure was 1/2546 (0.0%) with the same rate of vaginal cancer. There were no sarcomas noted. The most common type of bladder cancer associated with the presence of a foreign body is squamous cell carcinoma. Based on the findings, with a mean follow-up of almost four years the study did not support an association between polypropylene mesh used for midurethal slings and the development of malignancy in humans.

Yet, there have been few studies conducted and the question keeps being raised. Only time will tell whether there is a future link. If a link is established the 10-year long-stop limitation period will still apply.

Breast implants in France carry a warning after France's National Cancer Institute found a "clear link" between silicone implants and anaplastic large cell lymphoma (ALCL). There is developing research into the relationship between ALCL and breast implants. BAPRAS has stated that it supports the MHRA in exploring links between breast implants and ALCL. They suggest that members must warn prospective patients of the potential risk when counselling them and provide both verbal and written information.

It is estimated that between 5 and 10 million women have breast implants. Since the initial MHRA medical device alert in the UK in 2011 only fourteen cases of Anaplastic Large Cell Lymphoma (ALCL) have been reported (correct at March 2016). This may be due to the rarity of a diagnosis of ALCL (believed to be in the order of 1:50,000-300,000) or because it is not being reported to the MHRA as often as it should. A worldwide collaboration is required to provide robust data to investigate the link and BAPRAS' have stated their commitment to the

International Collaboration on Breast Registry Activities (ICOBRA).

BIA-ALCL is a lymphoma and not cancer of the breast tissue. When breast implants are placed in the body, they are inserted behind the breast tissue or under the chest muscle. Over time, a fibrous scar called a capsule develops around the implant, separating it from the rest of the breast. In women with breast implants, the ALCL was generally found adjacent to the implant itself and contained within the fibrous capsule. There is then rapid swelling of one breast and it is diagnosed on cytology of the periprosthetic fluid and the CD30 cell count in particular. Textured breast implants seem to carry a higher risk regardless of manufacturer. Whilst current advice is to inform patients of the risk but continue to use implants, there is no requirement to routinely remove breast implants as a matter of course.

Raw Materials

The origin of the raw materials of implants can raise concern. Since the PIP Implants used non-medical grade silicone, the possibility that contaminated raw materials can enter the market, knowingly or accidentally, is of great concern. Presently, federal prosecutors in the US are convening a grand jury to consider evidence that Boston Scientific used defective counterfeit raw materials from China for its devices.

A grand jury in Charleston, WV, has sent out multiple subpoenas recently seeking documents about Boston Scientific's purchase of a type of synthetic resin used in mesh implants, *The Boston Globe* has reported. Investigators in the U.S. Department of Justice (DOJ) want to see if the Marlborough, MA-based company knowingly got substandard resins from China that were cloaked in materials approved by regulators, and then sold them to healthcare providers.

Silimed are presently under investigation for the contamination of their breast implants. In October 2015 the MHRA recommended that no Silimed Silicone Implants be used following reports of contamination. Silimed is the 3rd largest implant manufacturer in the world exporting its devices to more than 75 countries worldwide. Eurosurgical a company which distributes Silimed's products in Britain, said it had supplied around 13,000 implants in the UK over the past 5 years. Silimed's products included breast, penile and testicular implants. The Company stated that the contamination was detected during an audit of the company's manufacturing practices. The outcome of this investigation is still awaited despite the German notified body finding contamination on some implants during an inspection at the company's manufacturing plant in Brazil. The contamination was from particles and fibres which should not have been there.

Knowing where the raw materials come from, sourcing medical grade supplies and protecting them from contamination is crucial to patient safety. A product liability case is highly likely to succeed if it can be shown that the products were substandard. However, manufacturers may put profit before safety and factor in the cost of a percentage failure rate and resulting litigation into the price of the product. Stopping manufacture and delaying product shipment impacts on their market placement and maintaining trade is often more important, as with the PIP Implants.

CONCLUSIONS

- Adverse incidents reported to MHRA and National Reporting & Learning System (NRLS) give an indication of the type of common complications associated with implants. There have been few reports compared to the number of surgeries.
- The MHRA and other regulatory bodies in the EU should be checked and the Yellow card reporting used by patients who have an adverse incident.
- Further work needs to be done to characterise long-term safety in relation to different surgical procedures and implant types.
- Informed consent, failure to provide alternative treatments and surgery errors form the basis of the majority of cosmetic surgery adverse events and complications.
- If there was a concern highlighted in another member state, the UK would be involved immediately to alert clinicians and manufacturers. Guidance would follow.
- A system of unique device identification (UDI) will assist patients and future research into safety of products.
- Some reported accounts show that the impact on the quality of life for some patients is severe.
- Literature suggests that some groups of patients may be more susceptible than others in developing adverse events or that surgical expertise and experience and patient aftercare may play a key role in reducing adverse events.
- Currently there is no national registry in the UK for implants. Discussion on a national registry is ongoing between NHS England and the specialised societies and MHRA.

- NHS Choices website, NICE guidance and specialist professional clinical websites provide comprehensive information for patients

Work is needed to improve reporting of adverse events and safety of certain devices and procedures. Better regulation of the industry as a whole is needed. Improved reporting may reveal future issues to which manufacturers and patients need to be alert.

Clinically, patients need to be carefully selected, counselled, and informed of all risks and complications in order to consent and have the benefit of a multi-disciplinary team of experienced professionals if needed.

Despite cosmetic surgery being a multi-million pound industry with slick advertising encouraging people to undertake procedures which are 'quick' and that you can practically 'do in your lunch hour', many patients do not fully grasp the gravity or potential risks of these operations and treatments. It is surgery that needs to be taken seriously. It is decision for life. In cosmetic surgery claims, inappropriate surgery is a common allegation. Followed by issues surrounding consent, postoperative care and choice of procedure. As the number and type of cosmetic procedures increases so will the number of providers. Until they understand and adhere to their legal and professional responsibilities, cosmetic surgery claims will continue to be a source of work for solicitors.

MORE BOOKS BY LAW BRIEF PUBLISHING

'Ellis and Kevan on Credit Hire, 5th Edition' by Aidan Ellis & Tim Kevan

'RTA Allegations of Fraud in a Post-Jackson Era: The Handbook, 2nd Edition' by Andrew Mckie

'A Practical Guide to Holiday Sickness Claims' by Andrew Mckie & Ian Skeate

'RTA Personal Injury Claims: A Practical Guide Post-Jackson' by Andrew Mckie

'On Experts: CPR35 for Lawyers and Experts' by David Boyle

'A Practical Guide to Claims Arising From Accidents Abroad and Travel Claims' by Andrew Mckie & Ian Skeate

'A Practical Guide to Claims Arising from Fatal Accidents' by James Patience

'A Practical Approach to Clinical Negligence Post-Jackson' by Geoffrey Simpson-Scott

'A Practical Guide to Personal Injury Trusts' by Alan Robinson

'Occupiers, Highways and Defective Premises Claims: A Practical Guide Post-Jackson' by Andrew Mckie

'Employers' Liability Claims: A Practical Guide Post-Jackson' by Andrew Mckie

'A Practical Guide to Subtle Brain Injury Claims' by Pankaj Madan

'The Law of Driverless Cars: An Introduction' by Alex Glassbrook

'A Practical Guide to Costs in Personal Injury Cases' by Matthew Hoe
'A Practical Guide to Alternative Dispute Resolution in Personal Injury Claims – Getting the Most Out of ADR Post-Jackson' by Peter Causton, Nichola Evans, James Arrowsmith
'A Practical Guide to Personal Injuries in Sport' by Adam Walker & Patricia Leonard
'A Practical Guide to Marketing for Lawyers' by Catherine Bailey & Jennet Ingram
'Baby Steps: A Guide to Maternity Leave and Maternity Pay' by Leah Waller
'The Queen's Counsel Lawyer's Omnibus: 20 Years of Cartoons from the Times 1993-2013' by Alex Steuart Williams

These books and more are available to order online direct from the publisher at www.lawbriefpublishing.com, where you can also read free sample chapters. For any queries, contact us on 0844 587 2383 or mail@lawbriefpublishing.com.

Our books are also usually in stock at www.amazon.co.uk with free next day delivery for Prime members, and at good legal bookshops such as Hammicks and Wildy & Sons.

We are regularly launching new books in our series of practical day-to-day practitioners' guides. Visit our website and join our free newsletter to be kept informed.

www.ingramcontent.com/pod-product-compliance
Lightning Source LLC
LaVergne TN
LVHW022055200926
848481LV00003B/917
* 9 7 8 1 9 1 1 0 3 5 2 7 5 *